Democratic Citizenship in Schools:
Teaching Controversial Issues, Traditions and Accountability

Also of interest:

Lyn Tett: *Community Education, Learning and Development*
(3rd Edition, 2010)

and

Policy and Practice in Education (series)

See www.dunedinacademicpress.co.uk for all our publications

Democratic Citizenship in Schools

Teaching Controversial Issues, Traditions and Accountability

Edited by

Jane Brown, Hamish Ross and Pamela Munn
Moray House School of Education, University of Edinburgh

EDINBURGH ◆ LONDON

First published in 2012 by
Dunedin Academic Press Ltd

Head Office
Hudson House
8 Albany Street
Edinburgh
EH1 3QB

London Office
The Towers,
54 Vartry Road,
London
N15 6PU
UK

ISBN 978-1-78046-005-5
© 2012 Dunedin Academic Press
The right of Jane Brown, Hamish Ross and Pamela Munn and the
contributors to be identified as the authors of this book has been asserted
by them in accordance with sections 77 & 78 of the Copyright, Designs
and Patents Act 1988

British Library Cataloguing in Publication Data
A catalogue record for this book is available from the British Library

Typeset by Makar Publishing Production
Printed by CPI Group (UK) Ltd., Croydon, CR0 4YY

Contents

Part III—Accountability

Acknowledgements

This book is based on an international seminar series at the University of Edinburgh organised by the newly formed *Citizenship and Democracy Network* of the Scottish Educational Research Association. The series was generously sponsored and supported by the Gordon Cook Foundation. We wish to thank everyone who participated in initial planning meetings for the series including Margaret Arnott, Alan Britton, Paula Cowan, Ross Deuchar, Lisa Hannah, George Meldrum, Margaret Petrie, Linda-Jane Simpson and Henry Maitles. The meetings identified the three substantive themes for the series and the central topics of democratic schooling, teaching controversial issues and accountability remain, forming the organising principle of this edited collection of papers.

This book is the outcome of an ongoing dialogue regarding education for citizenship with a group of researchers, policy makers and practitioners committed to the field, over many years. It is therefore appropriate to thank everyone who took part in the *Citizenship and Democracy* groups under the auspices of the Applied Educational Research Scheme (2004–9), which was funded by the Scottish Government and the Funding Council. We are especially grateful to Caroline Maloney who has provided excellent administrative support throughout. We also wish to thank Lesley Scullion for her input. Finally, we very much enjoyed working with our contributors. Many thanks to you all.

Contributors

Alan Britton was Stevenson Lecturer in Citizenship at the University of Glasgow and now works within the Education for Global Citizenship Unit at the School of Education in Glasgow. He was previously a secondary school teacher and the first Education Officer at the Scottish Parliament.

Jane Brown is a Senior Research Fellow at Moray House School of Education, University of Edinburgh. She has undertaken research in the field of education for citizenship and violence in schools over many years.

Kenneth Greer is Fife Council's Executive Director (Education). He taught in Scottish schools for 14 years before being appointed as Grampian Region's Adviser in English. He spent 10 years as one of HM Inspectors of Education, working as National Specialist in English and District Inspector.

Carole Hahn is the Charles Howard Candler Professor of Educational Studies at Emory University, Atlanta, USA. She has conducted numerous studies of citizenship education, written about civic education in the USA and comparatively, for which she received the Jean Dresden Grambs Distinguished Career Research Award from the National Council for Social Studies.

Henry Maitles is Professor of Education at the University of the West of Scotland. He researches, teaches and publishes in the area of citizenship, including the impact of citizenship initiatives in schools. He was a member of the Scottish Executive Review Group which drew up the proposals for education for citizenship in Scotland.

Gary McCulloch is Brian Simon Professor of the History of Education at the Institute of Education, University of London. His recent publications include *The Struggle for the History of Education* (Routledge, 2011) and *Cyril Norwood and the Ideal of Secondary Education* (Palgrave Macmillan, 2007).

Lejf Moos is Professor at The Institute of Education, Aarhus University, Copenhagen. He has been researching school leadership in Denmark and internationally for a number of years and has published extensively in the area.

Pamela Munn is Professor Emerita at the University of Edinburgh. A former Dean of the Moray House School of Education, she chaired the national group on Education for Citizenship in Scotland.

Daniel Murphy has been a local authority Adviser, Director of the Centre for Educational Leadership (University of Edinburgh) and a successful Headteacher. He is the joint author of *School Leadership* (Dunedin Academic Press, 2nd edn 2008).

Alison Peacock is Headteacher of the Wroxham Primary Teaching School and Leader of the Cambridge Primary Review National Network. Throughout her career she has recognised the transformative power of trust, inclusive pedagogy and co-agency.

Richard Pring was Professor of Educational Studies and Director of the Department at the University of Oxford from 1989 to 2003. From 2003 to 2009 he was Lead Director of the Nuffield Review of 14–19 Education and Training.

Hamish Ross is a lecturer in education at the Moray House School of Education at the University of Edinburgh. He has research interests in: representations of self, society, citizenship and environmental relations in the primary and secondary school curriculum; the development of agency and 'voice' in school contexts; and teacher attitudes to environmental and outdoor education.

Rita Verma completed her doctoral studies from the University of Wisconsin Madison. She is currently an Associate Professor and Program Director of Peace and Social Justice Studies at Adelphi University in New York. She has published numerous scholarly articles and books.

Introduction

According to the sociologist C. Wright Mills (1959), it is inescapable that every social issue is located within a particular ideological and historical moment. He argues that it is necessary to acknowledge how our behaviours and interests, as well as the actions of others, including governments, do not take place in a vacuum. As a consequence, Mills maintains our values are inevitably situated in a particular time and place. His insights can be borrowed to frame an understanding of the focus of this book, including the rationale for the selection of a specific thematic approach to its organisation:

- democratic schooling;
- teaching controversial issues;
- accountability.

The connections between these key themes come into sharp focus when 'citizenship' is understood as capturing the tensions of value *difference*, or the tensions between one ideological and historical moment and the next. Moreover, the idea that values are context-specific is not easy to reconcile with the liberal ideals that to some extent underpin efforts to establish global citizenships through, for example, international human rights (and 'rights of the child') agreements (cf. Waks, 2008).

This linked collection of papers is also located within the parameters of a particular historical moment and recognises its openness to ongoing change and innovation, not least in a period of intense globalisation. At the beginning of the twenty-first century nation states co-exist within an increasingly interdependent and connected world order that is unprecedented. Sustaining and invigorating political engagement in long-lived democracies is an ongoing and widespread concern, while emerging democracies are grappling with both establishing and safeguarding individual rights to participation (cf. Williams and Invernizzi, 2008).

Internationally, it is argued that a deepening crisis of legitimacy characterises the nature of the relationship between citizens and the key institutions which impact on their everyday lives (Gaventa, 2002). In addition, a globally travelling neoliberalism is influencing local education policy, emphasising efficiencies of competition and outcome measurement (Rizvi and Lingard, 2010). For both reasons, processes of **accountability** have permeated many levels of institutional life including schools and educational systems. At the same time, there are tensions between democratic accountability of schools to national citizenries, on the one hand, and processes of **democratic schooling** that seek to embed rights to participation, on the other. Such tensions can be seen at policy level, especially where new forms of citizenship are being invoked. Take the case of South Africa, where Waghid (2009) argues that the teaching of patriotism to break from an apartheid past might conflict with the desire to build a democratic future capable of including marginalised others.

Tensions often arise, too, around **controversial issues**, which are inevitable in citizenship according to Marshall (1950). Marshall's highly influential account maintained that 'citizenship' not only inscribed a *state of society*, but also a kind of *potential between* states of society—a difference between what might be ideal, and what was realised, in a given society at a given time—a driving force for (potentially) progressive transformation. His argument might be analysed by considering the meanings of citizenship as the eighteenth- and nineteenth-century period of European slavery came to an end, or in the contexts of the nineteenth- and early twentieth-century British suffragette movement, the late twentieth-century anti-apartheid successes in South Africa, or the early twenty-first-century 'Arab Spring'. How does schooling react at these times when difference is being negotiated? Marshall's own empirical evidence for this processual idea of 'citizenship' included the dialectical transformations and organised protests that resulted in social, economic and political change through the English industrial revolution. But still in established Western democracies, national schooling struggles to manage the paradoxical-seeming purpose—invoked by this understanding of citizenship—of *socialising young citizens as negotiators of social plurality* (e.g. Biesta, 2008). In the UK, the state-funding of schools that are organised by religious faith groups is one much-debated policy arena, upon which the inherent controversy of citizenship bears.

Seen like this, the intersections between processes of democratic schooling, the teaching of controversial issues and accountability to local or national democratic authority, are points where the research, policy and practice of citizenship education are open to fruitful scrutiny. In order to make such a case, first it is necessary to address critical and relatively recent innovations in conceptualisations of citizenship and the implications these have for the future of citizenship education more generally.

Conceptualising citizenship

How we understand citizenship has implications for how education for citizenship is conceived at the level of policy and framed and implemented in educational settings. Citizenship, however, is a value-laden and dynamic concept that has been the focus of longstanding controversies and argument. Traditionally the concept 'has been equated with membership of, and relationship with, nation state' (Lawson, 2001: p. 164). In Western thought this very influential account of citizenship has been couched in liberal terms, as an individual bestowed with a set of rights, obligations and responsibilities. In the past there has been a tendency to assume such 'liberal assimilationist' conceptions of citizenship (cf. Banks, 2008) have universal applicability. But this is rapidly changing. Today, transformative understandings of citizenship build on traditional understandings but are creating new ways of thinking about what it means to be an engaged citizen in an interconnected, global world (e.g. Lister, 2008). According to Waks (2008), a 'new cosmopolitanism' conceives citizenship in a way that draws not only upon liberal universalism, but also upon communitarian recognition of difference, moral situatedness, kinship and tradition. Strand (2009) stresses the radical ideal of the new cosmopolitanism, particularly in relation to promoting innovative forms of learning about the world as a global community. There are a number of identifying features in constituting cosmopolitanism. These relate to the self-perception of citizens and their place in the world community, their identification with significant global challenges (i.e. global warming, war and conflict), as well as their commitment to values such as equality and social justice (Lister, 2008; Banks, 2008).

The diversification of conceptions of citizenship in part attends the diminution of the role of the nation-state as the single custodian of citizenship, just as globalisation—as empirical fact and social imaginary—undermines the Westphalian conception of the absolute sovereignty of the state itself (Rizvi and Lingard, 2010). Moral-political issues such as climate change and food security have undermined the presumed efficacy of nation states acting alone, at least at the level of discourse where various kinds of collaborative, transnational partnerships are viewed as the solution to fixing complex global problems. In addition, significant social changes, in particular migration, the globalisation of the economy, nationalism and the rise of multicultural societies, have all influenced how we now understand the concept of citizenship (Banks, 2008; Benhabib, 2004) and, in some evidence, our dispositions towards cosmopolitanism (Mau *et al.*, 2008).

For instance, substantial numbers of individuals enjoy citizenship in one national setting while residing and working in another. Consequently the question of identity, including the multiple and complex nature of the allegiances of contemporary citizenship, is at the heart of contemporary debates about the meaning of citizenship (Lister, 2008). Pluralistic perspectives on citizenship, for example, tend to be less state orientated and stress the agency of citizens themselves (Gaventa, 2002). Today, citizenship is more likely to be regarded as both flexible and pluralistic, in part due to the fact that the allegiances of contemporary citizenship are increasingly more complex and involve multiple, mobile and hybrid identities (Audigier, 2000; Davies, 2008).

The rise of the human rights agenda in its various forms in the latter part of the last century has been a further important development which has led to a greater awareness and recognition of the position of marginalised and disenfranchised groups. The position of women and children are cases in point. In relation to children, the United Nations Convention on the Rights of the Child has done much to highlight the position of children in both the global South and North. In keeping with this international concern regarding the rights and wellbeing of children there has been a renewed academic interest in their ambiguous and differentiated status as citizens (cf. James, 2010). Is it possible to claim children and young people are citizens now, or are they aspiring citizen and 'citizens in the making' (Maitles and Gilchrist, 2005)?

The debate about what citizenship means is shifting towards developing models of citizenship which are both differentiated and multi-faceted.

Such ideas about citizenship tend to be underpinned by ideas about social justice, are more inclusive, participatory and stress 'active citizenship' (Jansen *et al.*, 2006; Lister, 2008) and are thus more amenable to recognising the positions of various identity-based and marginalised groups and their interests (Banks, 2008).

Rethinking education for citizenship

'Citizenship education must be re-imagined and transformed to effectively educate students to function in the 21st century' (Banks, 2008: p. 135). Banks is not alone in advocating that at the present moment marks a critical and important time for rethinking the scope and goals of education for citizenship.[1] As he suggests, alongside conceptual innovations in understandings of 'citizenship' is the way in which approaches towards, and rationales for, what we now call citizenship education have developed over the course of the twentieth century. This is readily illustrated in the changing vocabulary and practices of education for citizenship from 'civic instruction' and 'civic education' used widely in the early and mid twentieth century, to the more contemporary and familiar sounding: 'education for citizenship' used currently. In some European states the plurality of modern forms of citizenship is suggested by the use of the phrase 'education for citizenships' (Audigier, 2000).

More recently there has been a concerted attempt to address the nature of global citizenship education and what this term actually encompasses and what it would involve for schools. While the conventional goals of citizenship education were to build common identity, a shared history and encourage loyalty to the nation state (Lawson, 2001), today a formidable challenge is to put into practice educating for 'global citizenship' and managing the complex interplay between localised and nationally based citizenship identities with global citizenship (Davies, 2008).

Overview of this book and its approach

The approach of this book has two key dimensions. First, as indicated, we are taking a thematic approach to the topic of education for citizenship. The three themes of democratic schooling, teaching controversial issues and accountability were chosen because of their central relevance to citizenship education in the new millennium and we have highlighted a theoretical relationship between them above. In terms of the salience of democratic schooling, we know that how teachers act and behave in school and how democratic decision-making practices are modelled, and the way in which pupil understanding of diversity and difference is promoted, are critical experiences for young people, particularly those living in multicultural societies. In short, *how* citizenship is taught is as important as *what* is taught. Young people learn about citizenship in part through the experience of being part of a school community.

In terms of teaching controversial issues, it is established that this area is fundamental to the goals of education for citizenship, especially with regard to encouraging understanding of 'others' (see Verma in this volume). The challenge of teaching 'controversial issues' in a way that goes beyond somewhat sterile 'on the one hand … on the other hand …' approaches and engages young people in the complexities of modern life is formidable. Not only do teachers need to engage in a variety of approaches and activities to make topics 'come alive', but parents need to be aware of such teaching and support the engagement of young people in controversial issues as a legitimate part of schooling. This is all the more challenging in the current context of school accountability, which is the third theme of the book.

We know from research that schools are profoundly affected by the accountability criteria and procedures under which they operate. For example, accountability systems involving learners' examination grades encourage teachers to focus on borderline candidates in an attempt to increase the numbers achieving particular grades. Those at the bottom or top tend to receive less attention. More generally, teachers wanting to do the best for their students, study old examination papers and 'teach to the test'. Accountability systems send messages about what is and is not valued in the complex and multi-faceted job of learning and teaching. This poses a number of questions for citizenship education. Firstly, how can the effectiveness of citizenship education in schools be measured? Secondly, should young people's learning about citizenship be tested, and if so, what kind of learning should feature in tests? Thirdly, how can the importance of citizenship education be conveyed to schools, teachers, learners and their parents when citizenship does not feature in the entry qualifications to further and higher education – the common post-school destinations for students in advanced economies?

Finally, what if the accountability narrative itself is understood to be part of a neoliberal social imaginary of globalisation? Rizvi and Lingard (2006) have shown how the Organization for Economic Cooperation and Development (OECD) has become a policy player in precisely this respect by organising international comparisons of educational performance. If a neoliberal ideology dominates their very purposes, what can schools make of any citizenship education that works with contradicting imaginaries of globalisation—resistant to the neoliberal—such as those concerned with global injustice or environmental sustainability? Schools, as institutions with goals, specified purposes and tasks to achieve these goals, exist in a highly charged globalised environment where economic growth is seen as vital to the continued prosperity of people. 'Globalisation' is commonly used as a shorthand way of describing the spread and connectedness of production, communication and technologies across the world. That spread has involved the interlacing of economic and cultural activity (Smith and Doyle, 2002). The interconnectedness of economies and especially the speed by which capital flows around the world means that education has become a key area of public policy because it is seen as a very important engine of economic growth. Schooling as a key part of the education system is thus subject to intense scrutiny and control. A quick glance at any education policy document will reveal that a key purpose of education is economic prosperity. Indeed, Alison Wolf has suggested that we have almost forgotten that education ever had any purpose other than to promote growth (Wolf, 2002: p. xiii), such as the development of social equity. The now-dominant purpose of education policy, according to Rizvi and Lingard (2010), is to provide an educated, flexible and resourceful workforce ready to compete in this globalised economy. To take but one example, economic imperatives were highlighted in Education Secretary Michael Gove's announcement of the curriculum review in England:

> We have sunk in international league tables and the National Curriculum is substandard. Meanwhile the pace of economic and technological change is accelerating and our children are being left behind. The previous curriculum failed to prepare us for the future. We must change course. Our review will examine

the best school systems in the world and give us a world-class curriculum that will help teachers, parents and children know what children should learn at what age. (Department for Education, 2011)

This quotation highlights the political importance of international league tables, where young people's attainment in language, mathematics and science can be compared. How is education for citizenship to flourish in such a context?

Each of the three themes is introduced in more detail in section introductions. These short pieces by the editors summarise the key points being made and highlight areas and questions for discussion. In his concluding chapter Henry Maitles, who has worked extensively in the area of democratic schooling with young people, teachers and teacher educators, provides an insightful review of the state of understanding of citizenship education around the Western world, and the considerable challenges it faces. He uses UK experience as an illustrative reference point, stressing the need to maintain the momentum in this critical and important area.

The second key dimension in this collection is to include chapters from the perspective of research, policy and practice. Such an aim has a particular resonance in the field of education, where the need to promote connections between the worlds of research, policy and practice have been subject to intense scrutiny as well as criticism (Whitty, 2005). Education as an applied social science is predominantly concerned about impact. We know from research on policy making and from a series of debates and discussions (cf. www.sfre.ac.uk) that research is only one influence on policy making and that its influence is uneven. Similarly, the influence of policy on research agendas is limited, with little long-term investment in research in the UK on enduring educational issues. There is also a well-known gap between education policy on paper and classroom practice:

Education practitioners, policy-makers and researchers have been trapped in their parallel worlds, peering at each other from afar – but their knowledge about education makes an essential contribution to democratic debate and to informed judgement in policy and practice. (SFRE, 2010: p. 1)

This volume brings these perspectives into close proximity as a way of sharing knowledge and providing diverse resources for debating education for citizenship. The book is envisaged as a stimulus for discussion in staffrooms, seminars and policy forums.

Conclusion

Citizenship education is not only central to debates about the purposes of schooling. Its potential also lies in how it might deepen young people's views of some of the key challenges of our times. As this book makes clear, education for citizenship entails a great deal more than developing knowledge of political systems, promoting shared values and encouraging assimilation and integration. As well as strengthening young people's localised and national allegiances, it has the capacity to embrace and critically appreciate our globalised existence. Citizenship education is not merely a discrete subject field but integral to how we think about learning. It highlights traditional learning to be sure—the importance of a secure knowledge base founded on critical thought. It also recognises the importance of authentic learning, focusing on issues of direct contemporary importance and of active participation as a way of making learning meaningful.

Note
1 See Learning and Teaching Scotland .ltscotland.org.uk/learningteachingandassessment/ learningacrossthecurriculum/themesacrosslearning/globalcitizenship/

Part I

Democratic Schooling

Introduction to Part I: Democratic Schooling

The relationship between democratic schooling and citizenship is an important discussion that has yet to be fully embarked upon. In our introduction to this collection we drew attention to a deliberative openness in the concept of 'citizenship' over time. Similarly, in his 'meditation on democracy', Bernard Crick—chief architect of the (still precarious) existence of the school subject of 'citizenship' in England and Wales—described the word 'democracy' as both sacred and promiscuous (Crick, 2000b [1996]: p. 191). He drew attention to its mutability of meaning, through history, and to its tendency to substitute for the plurality and contestation that lies beneath: 'I do not find it helpful to call the system of government under which I live 'democratic'. To do so begs the question. It can close the door on discussion of how the actual system could be made more democratic ...' (Crick, 2000b [1996]: p. 193).

The three contributions in this section also have a shared recourse in history as they unpack the meanings of democratic schooling. McCulloch explicitly uses the study of historical debates as a central means of coming to terms with our present ideas about democratic schooling. Murphy adopts *past, present and future* as a device for examining democratic schooling even in the relatively culturally coherent case of a single small nation. Moos refers back to 'old wisdom' in his account of democratic schooling in the face of a more recent accountability narrative (see also Pring's extended discussion of democratic schooling in the themed section on *Accountability*).

There is a shared emphasis on how contested is the terrain of democratic schooling. Murphy uses examples from a wealth of experience to illustrate the complexities and contradictions of 'democratic values' like freedom, equality and fairness in school contexts. For example (and in an echo of elements of Plato's critique of Greek democracy as mob rule), he eventually asks whether the cultivation of an individual learner's right to hold an(y) opinion should trump the 'common search for truth' or 'the cultivation of a higher ideal of humanity'. Murphy's response—a kind of virtue ethics—opens up the question of the purposes of schooling.

Moos responds to a related tension: that between the democratic accountability of schools (outcomes) on the one hand, and democratic schooling, or schooling for democracy (deliberation), on the other. Murphy and Moos, in different ways, recognise the paradox that the school community's members must find ways of managing plurality and difference (among themselves) while holding a superordinate commitment to the community itself. It is to this problem in wider citizenries that democracy is a purported response. In setting up his consideration of democratic schooling 'between outcomes and deliberation', then, Moos draws on a Habermasian deliberative democracy and outlines some appropriate communicative strategies.

However, the possibilities of schooling with and for democratic values can be interrogated in less recent times according to McCulloch. Moos offers an account in which Western schooling has recently been affected by neo-liberal discourses of accountability, through *New Public Management* (Boston *et al.,* 1996), in which the concomitant trend towards teaching to a testing regime has damagingly individualist consequences. But for McCulloch *New Public Management* is the last element in his account of the democratic dynamics, symbolism and tensions of the expansion of education provision in the twentieth century and the attending relationships between private and public provision.

McCulloch's specific examples include the Association for Education in Citizenship, established in 1934; and experiments with democratic authority over schooling, such as A. S. Neill's Summerhill School (founded in 1924), and various attempts to assimilate private schools into a broader national system in the 1940s, and the greater centralisation of state education in England since the 1970s. What they reveal is that debate and contest over democratic schooling is not new. Moreover, there are aspects of the history of democratic schooling that might provide useful models, including of more collaborative and participative approaches to the management of the education system itself.

Key questions for this theme include:

- How can schools build communities that are both committed to the community and to the plurality of its members?
- How do accountability discourses interact with democratic schooling?
- What are the values and contradictions of 'democracy' that are revealed by the study of its evolution and practice in relation to schooling?

Historical Perspectives on Democratic Schooling

Gary McCulloch

Historical perspectives on democracy and education

John Dewey's famous remark 'What the best and wisest parent wants for his own child, that must the community want for all of its children' (Dewey 1899 / 1967: p. 7) has often been taken as the touchstone for democratic schooling. It is worth reminding ourselves first of all about what Dewey meant by this. He wanted to correct a tendency to look at schools 'from an individualistic standpoint, as something between teacher and pupil, or between teacher and parent', and to enlarge the range of the outlook to embrace the needs of the community as a whole. As he put it, 'Any other ideal for our schools is narrow and unlovely; acted upon, it destroys our democracy' (Dewey 1899 / 1967: p. 7). He went on to emphasise that this broader or social view was necessary in order to understand educational reforms. Otherwise, he argued:

> Changes in the school institution and tradition will be looked at as the arbitrary inventions of particular teachers, at the worst transitory fads, and at the best merely improvements in certain details—and this is the plane upon which it is too customary to consider school changes. (Dewey 1899 / 1967: p. 7)

Educational changes should, therefore, be understood in relation to 'larger changes in society' in order to comprehend them fully (Dewey 1899/1967: p. 8). Over the longer term, this meant assessing such changes historically, and Dewey explained how, for example, fundamental changes in industry over the past century had profound consequences for current school reforms.

One way of beginning to come to terms with debates around democratic schooling is to identify the historical ideals of democracy itself in relation to broader social, political and philosophical issues. This was usefully attempted by the late Bernard Crick (Crick, 2002, 2008). He had chaired the committee that produced a key report in Britain in 1998 on *Education for Citizenship and the Teaching of Democracy in Schools* (QCA, 1998), although, as he recognised, this report had provided no clear definition of democracy. Crick now proposed four broad historical usages of 'democracy'. The first was the critique of the ancient Greek philosopher Plato in which democracy meant the rule of the poor and ignorant over the educated, or mob rule, the anarchy of mere opinion over knowledge. The second, he associated with the Roman Republic, seventeenth-century English and Dutch republicans, and the early American republic: good government was mixed government under constitutional law, in which a democratic popular element could give greater power to a state. He related the third to the French Revolution and Rousseau, with the idea of the sovereignty of the people in which, regardless of education or property, everyone has the right to make their will felt in matters of state based on their own experience and conscience. Finally, he highlighted the Constitution of the United States and the new constitutions developed in the nineteenth and twentieth centuries in which everyone may exercise their rights to be active citizens but should also mutually respect the equal rights of fellow citizens within a regulatory legal order that defines, protects and limits those rights. As Crick pointed out, a historical approach is necessary partly in order to understand the nature of democracy itself as a changing and adaptable institution, and also because modern democratic ideas and systems have been developed in relation to their classical precedents (Crick, 2002: p. 3). Moreover, it demonstrates that the idea of democracy is far from a settled or agreed concept; as Robert A. Dahl has noted: 'The twenty-five centuries during which democracy has been discussed, debated, supported, attacked, ignored, established, practiced, destroyed, and then sometimes reestablished have not, it seems, produced agreement on some of the most fundamental questions about democracy' (Dahl, 1998: p. 3).

A historical perspective can also illuminate the often uneasy relationship between democratic ideals and social practice. The classic case here was

Alexis de Tocqueville who visited the USA in the 1830s. In his great work *Democracy in America* (De Tocqueville and Commager 1835–40 / 1946), De Tocqueville pointed out both the value of the 'absolute sovereignty of the majority' that he encountered there, and the dangers of what he described as the 'tyranny of the majority'. De Tocqueville found, however, that the prospect of such 'tyranny' was mitigated in the USA through the effective dispersal of power.

The issues raised by De Tocqueville are frequently discussed in terms of an ideal of 'liberal democracy'. The British political scientist Samuel Finer, for example, defined the characteristic features of liberal democracy as being a representative government in an elected legislature, a stabilising and expert executive accountable to these representative institutions, a system of social and economic checks and balances as a brake on the activity of the government, and a system of political checks and balances (Finer, 1970). According to Finer, Britain was 'an outstanding example of the liberal-democratic type of government' (Finer, 1970: p. 131). More recently, the American political scientist Amy Gutmann has expressed broadly similar ideals in an educational context. Gutmann's notion of democratic education is concerned with authority over education, which she argues should be shared between the state, parents and professional educators rather than being confined to, or dominated by, any one of these interests: 'The broad distribution of educational authority among citizens, parents, and professional educators supports the core value of democracy, conscious social reproduction in its most inclusive form' (Gutmann, 1987: p. 42).

If such general historical reflections on democracy can begin to inform debates about democratic schooling, an appraisal of the historical development of the education system can provide an important basis for our understanding. In this regard there are some key historical dynamics of the education system as it has developed that are essential to take into account. The first is the historical expansion of the education system in England over the past 150 years, and its relationship to the broader social and cultural context. During that time education has become a major feature in the national life. In quantitative terms, it has progressively involved increasing numbers of pupils at all levels, and more schools, teachers, universities and other educational institutions. It has also been increasingly recognised for its importance to society as well as to the economy (Aldrich, 2002). Because of its steady growth over the longer term, it has often been taken as a symbol and embodiment of democratic hopes and aspirations, and closely related to the process of political enfranchisement. Thus, for example, J. F. C. Harrison's history of the English adult education movement saw its central theme as 'the growth of democracy in England' (Harrison, 1961: p. xiv) and the contribution of education to this phenomenon.

Others, however, noted the problematic and contested nature of the relationship between education and democracy as it had developed historically. The English education system was oriented not only towards the growth of democracy but also towards capitalism and industry, which promoted a potential conflict between collective and individual interests. In the early 1960s, Raymond Williams explored a continuing and unresolved tension between private interests that would favour the 'free play of the market', and 'a public education designed to express and create the values of an educated democracy and a common culture' (Williams, 1961: p. 176). In the 1980s and 1990s, the educational reforms of the British Conservative Government seemed to many to have tipped the balance towards the competition of the free market and against democratic values. According to Carr and Hartnett, the English education system had never adapted to the growth of democracy. It had expanded to meet the needs of a democratic society, but 'the power of pre-democratic educational traditions and practices has continued to be felt' (Carr and Hartnett, 1996: p. 12). In this historical context, they argued, Conservative education policies represented 'a systematic attempt to reverse the historical trend towards a democratic and egalitarian society' in favour of 'individual freedom and *laissez-faire* economics' (Ranson, 1990; Carr and Hartnett, 1996: p. 11).

A second historical dynamic is between public and private forms of educational institution. In the nineteenth century, private agencies occupied a major position in the provision of education, both for working-class children and for the socially privileged. The latter were catered for through the independent or private schools, which charged fees to parents and were fiercely protective of their independence and privileges. As a public education system supported by the state developed in the late nineteenth and early twentieth centuries, the private sector developed separately and became increasingly antagonistic to potential threats to its status (Franklin and McCulloch, 2003). Under the Education Act of 1944, free secondary education became a universal right and obligation, extended to all up to the age of 15 in 1947 and up to 16 from 1972, but the private sector remained, and it continued to be associated with economic and social privilege. Increasingly, there appeared to be two separate education systems in England, one broadly accountable to the public and the other based on private interests, albeit highly diverse in its characteristics (Walford, 2003). There were many attempts to bring the public and private sectors together in some way, but these were generally unsuccessful (McCulloch, 2004). Recent and contemporary initiatives to develop a 'partnership' between the public and private sectors have had a powerful and resilient historical legacy with which to contend.

Thirdly, active state control over public education has grown greatly, especially over the past half century. For many years, the central authority presided more or less benevolently over a system that was based on a partnership between local education authorities, schools and teachers. In the 1920s, there was a long list of aspects for which the Board of Education had no formal responsibility, and it confined itself to 'superintendence' of a service whose administration and maintenance were largely local in nature (Selby-Bigge, 1927: p. 29). One keen observer, H. Bombas Smith, likened the English education system to a cricket club, which should have a constitution and recognised government and administration in order to achieve its common interests, but which would 'gain obedience by its moral authority, rather than by force'. Thus, he continued, 'His Majesty's Inspector will smoke his pipe with a headmaster and place his wider experience at his disposal in friendly conversation' (Smith, 1927: p. 49). After the Second World War, under the Ministry of Education, the state took a more active role in determining national policy, but maintained the ideal and tradition of a partnership in which teachers had a key role especially in the domain of the curriculum (McCulloch *et al.*, 2000; McCulloch, 2001).

Since the 'Great Debate' begun in Britain by the Labour Prime Minister James Callaghan in 1976, the state has extended the range of its active participation in public education, including the provision of a National Curriculum, national testing and assessment, greater accountability to parents, and the training of teachers. This was developed on the basis of seeking to achieve greater accountability to parents and the public in general for improving standards in the schools. The growth of centralised control over the education system could be supported in theory on the basis of democratic rationales, as it promoted greater accountability and uniformity across the national system and also gave greater scope for national priorities as determined by the elected government to be reflected in education. However, it also cut across ideals of liberal democracy such as had been represented in the previous partnership arrangement (McCulloch, 2011).

Against such a broad historical framework, we may begin to explore in more detail specific historical approaches to democratic schooling that may be of value in understanding the ideas and practices associated with education and democracy. It is important in doing so to appraise these critically in terms of their underlying assumptions, their positive contributions and the contradictions and problems that they reflect. Two historical examples of such approaches follow. First, the theme of education for citizenship and democracy is developed through the proposals of Sir Ernest Simon and the Association for Education in Citizenship (AEC) in Britain in the 1930s. Second, we explore further issues in the British post-war context relating to democratic authority and collaboration in schooling.

Education for citizenship and democracy
One of the key purposes of education in relation to democracy is as a means of promoting democratic values and virtues for future citizens. Dahl suggests that a basic criterion of a democratic process is enlightened understanding, so that 'within reasonable limits as to time, each member (citizen) must have equal and effective opportunities for learning about relevant alternative policies and their likely consequences' (Dahl, 1998: p. 185). He argues, moreover, that it has become imperative now, more than before, for democratic countries to improve the capacity of citizens to engage intelligently in political life, because of changes in scale due to increased internationalisation, the growth in the complexity of public affairs, and the increase in the amount of information available through a range of different media of communications (Dahl, 1998: p. 185). Yet this has been a persistent theme in the history of education. As Lundahl notes,

'Historically, the democratic functions of education have been placed high on the political agenda at times of rapid social change and upheaval' (Lundahl, 2002: p. 743).

In the 1930s, for example, education for citizenship and democracy was also a key issue, particularly due to the threat to democracy that was posed by the rise of fascist states and the prospect of war. In August 1939, on the eve of the Second World War, the Congress on Education for Democracy was convened in New York in front of a large international audience, in the conviction that 'No more important problem faces civilisation than the defence and advance of democracy; no more important problem faces America than the education of the citizen' (Congress on Education for Democracy, 1939: p. 1). It was these problems that Sir Ernest Simon sought to address in Britain through the establishment of the AEC in 1934 (McCulloch, 1994).

Sir Ernest Simon was an industrialist and former Liberal Member of Parliament who belonged to what Michael Bentley has described as the 'liberal intelligentsia' of the early twentieth century, representing a 'social elite' rather than a collection of intellectuals (Bentley, 1977: p. 161). His values were those of public service and leadership in relation to the fundamental principles of democracy, which he saw as 'the belief in government by discussion and consent rather than by force' (Simon, 1934). He had a somewhat elitist notion of this, as he argued that public opinion was prone to 'imbecility ... in times of excitement' and also that 'democracy does not depend for its validity on the wisdom of the popular vote' (Simon, 1934). He was confident that over the previous century, the power of the landed aristocracy had been removed in England, representing a 'bloodless victory for democracy'. Remaining injustices and inequalities would, in his view, be addressed 'to complete the social revolution by reason and goodwill and cooperation' (Simon, 1935a). The rise of authoritarian regimes on the Continent endangered not only the gains made in the past but also the prospects of further development, and he argued that it was therefore now necessary to place greater emphasis on education for citizenship than had been done before.

The AEC was thus established to help encourage the education system 'to fit the pupil for the public duties of citizenship in a democratic state' (Hubback and Simon, 1934: p. 5).

This was intended to promote a democratic remedy to the contemporary crisis of civilisation that would provide an alternative to the authoritarian remedy. Education was the key means of achieving this, and yet, according to Simon, 'we have never given any serious thought to education for citizenship of a democratic state; we are not giving nearly enough education, nor is it generally of the right kind' (Simon, 1935b: p. 5). The education of the day was inadequate for nearly all. Those who carried on in school did not always develop the qualities of citizenship, as the curriculum was too academic (Simon, 1935b: p. 6). Much of our education, Simon continued, was 'still completely detached from the problems of the modern world' (Simon, 1935b: p. 6). Indirect education for citizenship may have been enough in the nineteenth century, but now things have changed: 'The political world is so complex and difficult that it is essential to train men just as consciously and deliberately for their duties as citizens as for their vocation or profession' (Simon, 1935b: p. 7). In an educated democracy, Simon concluded, 'the voter should acquire a number of soundly based convictions on the main political questions of the day' and have the capacity 'to choose a good representative and to trust him when chosen' (Simon, 1935b: p. 9).

The AEC thus represented and sought to promote a significant set of democratic values through educational means, and deserves recognition for this, especially as a liberal response to the political and social crises of its time. Nevertheless, it was hardly democratic in its own approach, in that it was led by a small elite group that sought wider influence through persuading politicians and policy makers in its own elevated social circles. The Board of Education's consultative committee was investigating the problems of secondary education under the chairmanship of Sir Will Spens, and Simon was able to pursue both the chairman of the committee and the permanent secretary of the Board of Education personally on behalf of his own agenda (Spens, 1938). The Spens Report, published in 1938, ultimately accepted that, 'On the extent to which the youth of this country can be fitted to fulfil later their duties, and to take advantage of their opportunities, as citizens of a democratic State may well turn the whole future of democracy, and that not only in this island' (Board of Education, 1938: p. xxxvi).

A further set of contradictions in relation to the AEC was that it found support for its educational activities chiefly from the head teachers of progressive independent, fee-paying schools in the private sector which catered mainly for the socially privileged. These included Thorold Coade at Bryanston in Dorset, and F. Crossfield Happold, Head of Bishop Wordsworth's School in Salisbury (Watkins, 2006). In common with most members of the social elite, Simon sent his own sons to an independent school, Gresham's School in Holt, Norfolk, which had a reputation at this time for promoting advanced ideals in citizenship. There was a further tension in relation to Gresham's, as it enforced a 'moral supervision' of its pupils in the form of an honour system which extended 'to the most intimate details of their private lives' (Simpson, 1925: p. 84). The headmaster of Gresham's, J. R. Eccles, expressed his pride in his memoirs about the 'liberty' allowed to boys at the school, that is, 'to boys who could be trusted not to abuse it' (Eccles, 1948: p. 33). However, at least one future poet who was a pupil at the school, W. H. Auden, was not convinced, complaining dramatically: 'The best reason I have for opposing Fascism is that at school I lived in a Fascist state' (Auden, 1934 / 1984: p. 9; McCulloch and Woodin, 2010).

Democratic authority over schooling

The second historical example to be examined here relates to that of democratic authority in education. There are a number of issues involved in this, first about schools as democratic institutions, secondly the nature of political authority over schools, and thirdly the extent of state activity in the area of schooling as a whole.

With regard to the first of these, schools as democratic institutions, historically a number of initiatives to promote a democratic role for pupils and students have been in the independent or private sector as opposed to the public sector. Summerhill School, founded by A. S. Neill in England in 1924, and Sudbury Valley School, founded in Framingham, Massachusetts, in 1968, are widely known and sustained attempts to develop a strong notion of participative democracy for the pupils in the context of an independent school (Croall, 1983; Trafford, 2008). There have also been interesting cases in the public sector which are attracting increasing attention from historians of education, for example St George-in-the-East Secondary School in Stepney, London, Countesthorpe Community College in Leicestershire and Stantonbury Campus in Milton

Keynes (Watts, 1977; Fielding, 2009). For all that, it does appear that, as Limage emphasises, even in countries that consider themselves democratic in their political processes, schooling has been, as it still remains, 'a place where learning the practice of democracy is the exception, rather than the rule' (Limage, 2001: p. xxii).

In the second case, political authority over schools, we find an area rich in ambiguity so far as democratic issues are concerned. In England at least, historically this has often been a matter of attempting to assimilate private schools into a more broadly accountable system of education. The sympathies of Sir Cyril Norwood at the start of the Second World War for some accommodation between the maintained system and public schools in order to provide what he called 'the single national system of the future which will make democracy not unequal to the task' (Norwood, 1940) were dismissed out of hand by Lord Hugh Cecil, the provost of Eton College, as 'pure Totalitarianism' (Cecil, 1940; McCulloch, 2007). At the same time, the educational reformer R. H. Tawney could not understand why the assertion of LEA control would necessarily impair the freedom of independent schools (Tawney, 1943). These were tensions that were to remain live and potent in a changing social and political context well after the Second World War.

In terms of the third issue raised here, the state's authority over the education system, as has already been seen, in the English context this had grown markedly in a number of directions since the 1940s and especially since the 1970s. This may be viewed as the growth of a command-and-control model of central authority in which power is concentrated at the centre, as opposed to collaborative or dispersed models in which power is shared with partners. A number of approaches have been proposed as alternatives to centralisation. Burgess (1980), for example, suggested that remedies to the problems of education 'from the top down', involving an increase in the centralised direction and control of what is taught and how it is assessed, were insufficient in themselves (Burgess, 1980: p. 6). This view has some similarities with the historical analysis of Tyack and Cuban in the United States, who have suggested that educational changes along the grain of collaborative teacher cultures have been more enduring than top-down initiatives, although they describe these participative movements as being 'from the inside out, a kind of adaptive tinkering that preserves what is valuable and remedies what is not' (Tyack and Cuban, 1995: p. 136; Franklin *et al.*, 2003).

Conclusions

Historical perspectives are themselves contestable; and there are undoubtedly many other aspects of long-term social change and conceptions of democracy that this chapter has not addressed. Addressing historical concerns in this way is also not intended to convey a message that we can draw straightforward historical lessons that are simple and unproblematic. They should begin to provide a basis for a historical contribution to this profoundly important theme. Viewed in this light, historical debates around democracy and democratic schooling are fundamental to an understanding of contemporary issues in this area.

The more detailed historical examples around education for citizenship and democracy and democratic authority in education may also have a lasting value. The former reminds us of the importance of education in the fostering of citizenship and democracy, of some of the ways in which this role can be conceived, of the special resonance of this approach at times of social change and threat, and also of the assumptions, shortcomings and contradictions involved even in well-meaning and principled educational initiatives. The latter highlights a historical and ongoing debate about the democratic implications of centralised control over schooling. It also suggests the potential for a renewed understanding of alternative approaches involving greater collaboration and partnership that have a presence in our past. Indeed, a less controlling and more coherent approach on the part of the state might be not only more efficient than many of the educational reforms developed over the past generation, but also a more effective means of promoting the cause of democratic schooling.

Democratic Schooling in Scotland:
Past, Present and Future

Danny Murphy

In this chapter 'democratic' will not be defined narrowly with reference to particular political structures or systems. David Halpern's insider analysis of the operations of central government in the UK in the first few years of the twenty-first century, which presents us with an image of a liberal paternalistic state, conscious of the 'economy of regard', with media savvy campaigns and 'nudging' interventions, demonstrates very clearly how multi-layered contemporary 'democracy' is (Halpern, 2010). This chapter is situated within the similarly complex Scottish democratic context and should be read with reference to three broad 'democratic values' which flow in, through and around concepts, systems and institutions of democracy—fairness, equality and freedom. These are neither simple in themselves, nor in relationship to each other. Increases in freedom can, for example, reduce equality, while the imposition of equality can excessively restrict freedom and be seen, consequently, as unfair. They are important values in relation to 'schooling'—an active concept, which carries implications of 'training', 'directing down a particular path', but also important in relation to the broader, more open-ended concept of 'educating'. Examples of schooling will be drawn from my experience in secondary schools in contemporary Scotland. Often it is in secondary schools that the greatest challenges in balancing freedom and equality are to be found. These examples bring the underlying issues and values into individual focus. This chapter is not designed to be comprehensive, but to stimulate thinking through the use of examples—policies, systems, schools, events. As its title suggests, it is divided into three main sections illustrating the character of democratic schooling in Scotland.

Democratic schooling in Scotland: past

Education in Scotland, aspects of which had a meritocratic character, has been a source of pride for many Scots in the past:

> Other countries may have shown a finer flower of scholarship, but in none has the attitude towards education been so democratic, so thoroughly imbued with the belief that learning is for the whole people, so socialised as to afford the spectacle of the sons of the laird, the minister, and the ploughman, seated on the same bench, taught the same lessons, and disciplined with the same strip of leather. In no other country has there been in the past the same free path for ability, in whatever rank produced, not only through the schools, but into all the learned professions ... (Gibson, 1912, quoted in Anderson, 1985: p. 82)

While Robert Anderson's scholarship has introduced a welcome uncertainty into such 'rosy tinted' understandings of the Scottish educational pedigree, it does appear that reference to a Scottish educational 'tradition', whether or not the reality matched up, has played an important role in Scotland's distinctive educational history. Lindsay Paterson's excellent account of developments in the twentieth century explains how the evolutionary change which led to massive, accessible schooling opportunities for all, was shaped distinctively in Scotland, at least in part, by the institutional legacy of previous centuries and the constant reinvention of the inherited 'ideals' of Scottish education (Paterson, 2003): ideals among which freedom, equality and fairness loomed large.

Paterson rightly gives prominence to the Advisory Council on Education in Scotland, whose visionary 1947 report laid out a template for democratic schooling. Just as impressive was the inspirational vision of Aneurin Bevan, envisaging the beginning of a new educational era, in which the different school systems of the United Kingdom would equip every young person for their role in the democracy of the future. Speaking at the end of the Second World War, with all the ambition to create a new and better world that characterised that period, he gave powerful expression to the important role schools might play in democratic formation:

... for the first time in history the common man steps on the stage. We insist that education is primarily concerned with the ordinary person, and not with the exceptional person. The ordinary person is asked to decide issues of far greater gravity than any exceptional person in the past ... These boys and girls are to be asked to wield the royal sceptre; we must give therefore give them the souls of kings and queens. Otherwise it may be said that we took the ordinary man from the shadows of history and set him in the fierce light that beats upon thrones and he was blinded and ran away. (quoted in Barker, 1986: p. 8)

In secondary schooling in the second half of the twentieth century, the most significant development in this direction was the establishment of comprehensive schools, institutions which were intended to deliver the aspirations of the Advisory Council and of Bevan, offering equal access to a broad, balanced curriculum for all Scottish young people up to at least age 16 (from 1972). The initial introduction of comprehensive education was accompanied in many places by the construction of all-purpose schools with up-to-date facilities, large enough to offer a wide variety of certificated courses to all. Bruce Millan, Secretary of State for Scotland, recognised that schooling all young people in the same building was not the same as meeting the ideals of comprehensive education:

Certification is no good if the lower levels are seen to be 'valueless' ... you will really have the danger, the great danger that you really will begin to categorise pupils again ... the important thing is to try and develop courses for the less academically inclined pupil, in the first instance; that is the glaring deficiency of the comprehensive school at the moment. (McPherson and Raab, 1988: pp. 309–10)

However, delivering a curriculum which did not 'categorise' or 'grade' pupils according to their accomplishments in examinations proved much more difficult than delivering buildings. The Scottish Education Department (SED) saw the S3/S4 (ages 14–16 approximately) curriculum as the key area in which to deliver a more equal experience for all school students. Taking account of the extensive public consultation which followed the Munn (SED, 1977a) and Dunning (SED, 1977b) reports,[1] the SED in the early 1980s introduced the 'Standard Grade' programme, offering all Scotland's young people a broad balanced curriculum, attainments in which would be certificated within three broad levels: Foundation, General and Credit. The aspiration of Standard Grade was to provide opportunities for every individual in Scotland to have their achievements recognised. However, it ranked pupils and, after the introduction of exam targets for schools, the schools themselves, on a linear scale of academic value, according to the numbers and quality of awards attained. The system is still in operation and will eventually be phased out in 2014.

As a headteacher, I regularly talked with talented young people who lacked the skills to succeed at Credit Level and who saw no value in a Foundation award. Their perception was often of an unfair system which forced them into a comparative ranking with much more capable peers. For some pupils this was profoundly demotivating. However, where the school made clear that the community valued each individual, irrespective of academic ability, and where teachers developed good personal relationships with their students, this could go some way to restoring motivation. As one girl summarised her feelings to me: 'The only reason I do the work in this class is because I like the teacher. She obviously wants me to do well so I give it a go for her . . . but I'm not really bothered'.

The gap between the aspiration of Standard Grade and the experience of many such pupils in Scottish schools illustrates tensions across the underlying values of Scotland's schooling system: valuing each individual but giving an apparently higher value to the more academically able; offering equality of opportunity, but providing some with more 'credit' to cash in on their individual journey than others; comprehensive inclusive schooling from which those attending independent schools are excluded.

I have argued elsewhere (Murphy, 2007) that these value conflicts reflect the social complexity of our day-to-day world of relationships and shared endeavour, a fragmented plural social world represented in increasingly individual ways in an individualising society through distinctive individual cognitive maps of the world, distinctive values frames and personal intentions and emotional affections. Value conflicts are often hidden beneath the urgent fudges and compromises of political decision-making, as illustrated very clearly in Paterson's account of educational reform in Scotland between 1965 and the 1980s (Paterson, 2003: pp. 136–42).

Some schooling systems from the past were clearer about purpose and meaning. This was obviously the case for Church schools in Scotland, whose primary mission was value-based.[2] Not always articulated, but clear in actions and symbols is the civic mission of the American classroom (Johnson 1980). We see it in the moving commitment of French schoolteachers in the early years of the Third Republic, determined to instil the kinds of civic virtues which would prevent another Napoleon seizing power (Ozouf, 1967). We can see it in the 'civilising' mission of the Scottish primary school teacher in the depressed 1930s (Bowie, 1975). We can see it in the educational mission of a 'post-conflict society' in Kosovo (Goddard, 2004). The legacy of the Scottish past to its state comprehensive schools is a less direct, more uncertain, educational mission. Schools operate within a broad, messy institutional and policy framework, within which teachers and students in individual school communities create their own patterns of meaning and relationships, such as those between the student quoted above and her teacher.

Democratic schooling: present

In the present, the exciting energetic daily life a typical Scottish secondary school amply illustrates this interplay of democratic values and their impact on the lives and understanding of individuals, so examples from school life are used in this section to bring the broader issues into vivid relief.

A school responded to the increasing use of sophisticated mobile phones by conducting a community wide debate in which the various advantages and concerns of their use in school were aired—in Parent Forums, in Student Council, in staff meetings, in Assemblies. Following this debate, a new policy was agreed to replace the previous unworkable policy in which phones had been completely 'banned'. The new policy stated that pupils were permitted to use their phones in social areas outwith the timetabled school day but there was a strict sanction (confiscation and return to the parent, not the pupil) if a phone were to be used in the classroom.

Shortly after the introduction of the new policy, one of the Depute Headteachers was called to a science laboratory by a teacher. She found an argument taking place as a 14-year-old girl had refused to hand over her mobile phone, which she had been using under the desk in class. She had also refused either to leave the room in order to discuss this with the teacher in a less confrontational one-to-one setting or to report to the Depute Head herself. There was a great deal of emotional heat in the room. The learning objective of the lesson (to learn how to balance simple neutralisation equations) had been lost some time ago. Later, after investigation and discussion of the incident with the girl, and eventually her mother, both the girl and her mother justified her disruptive behaviour on the grounds that she needed to have her phone, no matter what the school policy said ('freedom') and that her treatment had been 'unfair', since another girl had already used her phone in the class and the teacher had 'done nothing about it'. The teacher 'doesn't like me anyway'. To what neutral agreed ground for resolution can the conversation refer, when democratic values can be interpreted to such different purpose? For the girl and her mother, individual freedom is more important than 'schooling'.

What would Bevan have made of the girl clinging to her mobile phone, and resisting the arbitrary power of the school as an instrument of state oppression? Indeed, this is the perceived character of schooling for a significant number of our young people and their parents. Schooling is something done 'to you', not 'with you', by people who drive in from somewhere else. School is an experience which you are compelled into; which you may, at best, tolerate, in among the more exciting aspects of your teenage years; these 'scholars' find school alien. It is a place where they come, as a colleague of mine once wryly observed, 'to watch adults working hard', before getting on with their lives. Asked to do homework in order to improve their chances in national examinations, some refuse, making clear that while the teacher can have some authority over them between 9 and 4, the evenings and weekends are *their* time. Such pupils may feel shut out of full participation ('Credit' level courses, progression on to S6[3]), by lack of skills in formal language and in decentred modes of thinking, and react accordingly by rejecting, or at best passively tolerating, the system which they see as rejecting them. This is not the whole picture of contemporary schooling, but it is the picture of many of the 20% which the OECD report of 2007 (OECD, 2007) recommended should get a better deal out of the

Scottish school system. Where are the values of 'freedom', 'equality' and 'fairness' played out in such exchanges?

Contemporary Scottish democratic (secondary) schooling can be conceived of as schooling *for* democracy; schooling *as* democracy and schooling *in a* democracy. My experience as a secondary school headteacher is that a lot of the purpose and activity of schooling *for* democracy is schooling *as* democracy. Teaching 'civics' in a comprehensive school in the early 1980s, I, as the 'authority', aimed to interest students, usually unsuccessfully, in the structures and systems of UK and European democratic institutions. As a headteacher in the 2000s, I realised that 'democratic formation' is as multi-layered and complex as democracy itself: knowledge of institutions is important for democratic formation, but just as important is the experience of a community which delivers 'fairness' through balancing 'freedom' and 'equality'.

In the school where I was headteacher, 15-minute weekly Assemblies (the first five minutes of which were given over to registration) were held in 'Houses' (350–400 pupils) since we could not assemble the entire school in any one space but still believed it to be important to bring as many students and staff together as possible, as a formal space in which individuals come to understand their broader community. House Captains (elected by their peers) spoke each week on matters of current concern; they might review the House position in the inter-House competition and the position of Tutor Groups in the 'tutor group of the month' competition, where various pro-social activities were encouraged and rewarded; a pupil whose family had recently immigrated from Eastern Europe might speak of things they have valued in coming to Scotland and things they have not liked; several pupils, from all stages and at all levels of academic performance, would receive 'success awards' having been nominated by their teachers for a very good display of citizenship or learning behaviours; announcements would be made of various opportunities to participate in the wider life of the school community beyond the classroom (a musical show, a dance group, library activities, sporting clubs, an educational trip being run by the Modern Languages teachers); the headteacher would raise areas of concern with movement around the building, which increase the risk of accidents, explaining the link between the rules for movement and reduction of risk. Delivery was snappy. The profile of those contributing (gender, age, academic profile, disability) represented the variety of the school.

This is a vibrant dynamic community, with lots of effective participation, responsible citizenship and successful learning.[4] The school is part way towards accreditation as one of UNICEF's 'Rights Respecting Schools'; part way towards Green Flag accreditation as an 'eco school'; citizenship activities are run through an ASDAN awards system; many pupils are engaged in community volunteering through the Duke of Edinburgh award scheme, and report on their experiences to the whole school; some pupils act as Young Sport Ambassadors, taking a leadership role in the development of sporting opportunities in the local area; senior pupils act as 'mentors' for younger pupils; 50 trained 'peer mediators' use skills of mediation and conflict resolution on a daily basis. In any given week, several of these groups, and others, may make presentations at the Assembly, representing back to their House as a whole the varied character of participation and achievement in the school community. On other days, morning tutorials provide a 'communicative space', where young people of different ages can share ideas and opinions and feed these in to the wider community both through representation (in Student Council) and through occasional 'megalogues' (Etzioni, 1997). These are dialogue involving the whole community on important issues for all: for example, the use of mobile phones! All teachers receive basic training in restorative practice, while the vast majority are fully trained in cooperative learning (with its strong emphasis on mutual support in learning) and in assessment for learning (using assessment to help children learn rather than to rank their attainment). There is a school complaints system for pupils who feel unfairly treated. The first option in any conflict is conflict resolution rather than imposed discipline. Pupils involved in disciplinary incidents can opt to deal with matters restoratively, or to 'choose known disciplinary consequences' if they prefer. A reasonably fair 'criminal justice' system deals with the fights, internet-generated conflicts and family disputes which are brought in the door, often on a Monday morning. Great emphasis is placed on forming honest, trusting relationships.

In the fragmenting and fragmented social world of 2012, the quality of the individual relationships that support the work of the school is highly important. Pupils are motivated to work, to learn, to see themselves as valued persons in the school community, at least in part by their perception of the teacher's view of them (McLean, 2009). All this takes place around the 'core business' of developing intellectual, emotional, physical and personal skills through classroom learning. These are kinds of routines typical of a Scottish comprehensive school in 2012. These routines are built around an understanding that many of our pupils cannot learn well through decentred academic disciplines, but do learn successfully where these are made real in their lives through experience and participation. In this way, schooling *for* democracy includes varied experiences of schooling *as* democracy.

It is in the day-to-day exchanges in the school that democratic values should be seen at work. Equality of respect is demanded if it is not given; restrictions on freedom are justified with reference to the need to restrain individual freedoms (for example, in the use of mobile phones) in the interests of the interdependent community; authority and power are exercised in accordance with agreed principles and properly held to account; there is a commitment to fairness in the way the institution handles competing claims.

It is, however, a costly process: instruction takes significantly less time than explanation. It can also fail: opening up dialogue may simply make clear the extent to which values differ. In our yearly questionnaires of pupils' perceptions of their schooling experience, the majority regularly told us that they did *not* feel all pupils are treated fairly. The perception of a significant majority of our pupils was that pupils who were 'badly behaved' were dealt with differently . . . and that 'the more badly behaved you are, the more you get away with'. One year, our Student Council, chaired by our Head Boy, took this issue to the local authority, so incensed were some of them that some of the worst-behaved pupils in the school were receiving extra rewards (free leisure activities, provided by the authority 'Community Learning Team', independently of the school, to young offenders). Issues of 'equality' and 'fairness' were to the fore in those discussions. 'We behave well and we don't get these special "treats"', they complained. The tensions of including everyone in the community, including those who would be classed as antisocial and possibly criminal, were evident on a daily basis—perhaps a good preparation for democratic living? Competing forces, sometimes causing confusion, uncertainty and tension in the schooling experience are not all then within the control of the school. If this character of contemporary democracy is replicated in the school, where is the space for 'schooling', directed activity which has specific goals? As a public institution within a democracy, the comprehensive school cannot insulate itself from these wider complexities in the way that more selective schools can. What then of 'schooling *in a* democracy'?

Who is in charge of schooling, for what purposes and within what framework of understanding? What should be the proper role of the teacher as a public professional, with the authority of expert knowledge, relative to the people's elected representatives?

Should teachers, for example, be able to participate in public debate on educational issues of concern (such public participation is currently a disciplinary offence)? Who is responsible for, and who is accountable for, the outcomes of democratic schooling? If local authorities, parents, pupils themselves, national government and its various agencies, teachers and headteachers are jointly responsible, then should they not be variously accountable for their own contributions, or should the accountability, as at present, sit with the school? In our current system, if there are problems, local authorities can blame national government for poor resourcing or confused priorities. National government can blame local authorities for poor implementation of national policy. Teachers blame headteachers for looking for too many different outcomes. Headteachers blame Inspectors (not in public usually) for setting out an uneven playing field. Teachers blame parents for expecting schools to do their job for them. Parents blame other parents or other children for not giving their child the space and time she or he needs:

> All in all our democratic schooling system appears to be a bit messy. These confusions make it difficult, in some cases, to develop the kinds of long term trusting relationships which are necessary for school communities to operate well. (Bryk and Schneider, 2002: p. 5)

However, despite this 'messiness', the majority of Scottish secondary schools, as reported by Inspectors, do appear to develop very strong trusting relationships with their parents and with most of their pupils, as evidenced by the generally favourable reports of Her Majesty's Inspectorate of Education (HMIE) on the quality of relationships in Scottish schools. There may be on the part of many parents a mature recognition that such complexity is part of the fabric of plural democratic life and that schools reflect that and deal with it in positive ways through 'building community' in the daily life of the school: that the daily actions that contribute to 'building community' are a powerful aspect of democratic schooling, but also represent a strong element of what schools contribute to building democracy. What then of the future?

Democratic schooling: future

Are we to hope for better democratic schooling in the future? There are certainly challenges—and not just for government, but for our democratic civic community. Core challenges include a number of clarifications. Where is the line that separates the teacher, as a public service professional, from a 'hired hand' whose job is to follow instructions within a service model? The Scottish Parliament Education and Lifelong Learning Committee recently consulted on the governance of schooling. Who is going to be responsible for which aspects of schooling and who will be accountable for the performance of schools? How should that performance be measured? Scotland's new *Curriculum for Excellence* provides criteria for judging schooling success which reach beyond examination performance to personal characteristics and capacities (Learning and Teaching Scotland, 2011). Can *Curriculum for Excellence* help improve democratic schooling? Although it has come in for some legitimate criticism in terms of its intellectual rigour, I believe that if the Experiences and Outcomes which now define the Scottish curriculum are taken as a minimal statement of the educational entitlement of every Scottish child up to age 15 (or 'Level 3'), it has much to commend it (Learning and Teaching Scotland, 2009). As currently proposed, the new curriculum allows development into more rigorous subject-based work. Better differentiated progression and less 'linear ranking' than the previous curriculum will require the development of appropriate pathways to 'positive destinations' at the end of the core curriculum phase (age 15).

Curriculum for Excellence also takes a wider view of the educational accomplishments and experiences we want schools to provide for every child than we have had before, aiming to cultivate the 'four capacities'.[5] I believe these will only be a sufficient preparation for full democratic living if they lead to education in, and cultivation of, certain civic virtues. If we lack agreed descriptions of moral values relevant to our democratic way of living, we offer only a thin description of human potential. What place do we give to honour, courage, honesty, nobility, charity, tolerance, respect for persons? I do not attempt here a definitive list of the democratic virtues to be cultivated, but I do argue that the inner life of the person, each as great in dignity as the next, is a valuable aspect of democratic formation and one too much neglected in recent years.

There also has to be some commitment to a joint educational project. In my experience, teachers, challenged by the emotivist language of many young people, often find that they have to acknowledge that entitlement to an opinion is more important than justification of the opinion. Acceptance of the 'right to opinion' trumps the search for truthful meaning—'before I even enter into a conversation with you, you must accept my absolute right to have the opinion I have'. If one person's opinion counts for more than a common search for truth, where can we find common ground? In the absence of some agreed description of such values and virtues of democratic living, democratic schooling may only create a space in which a relativist materialism provides a 'lowest social denominator'. This vision of democracy simply guards neutrality rather than cultivating a higher ideal of humanity.

While it is important to be 'good at' various accomplishments, these need to be for a good purpose; they need, in other words, to be harnessed and focused by positive values. In a confusing globalising plural world, common understandings of value and meaning derive from shared language and shared ways of knowing. I disagree with the proposition that because we cannot know the future, our curricular focus must therefore be on 'flexible skills'. Skills are important, but there is much we can learn from our past, much knowledge which has the authority of wisdom. Knowledge, understanding and skills are all required to sustain and support the continued flourishing of our democratic values. Knowledge, values and skills are in a necessary interdependent interrelationship, as outlined, for example in the Standard for Initial Teacher Education in Scotland (GTCS, 2006b). Teachers require the expert 'authority' needed to develop each aspect. Teachers are always more than 'facilitators'.

I have argued that *Curriculum for Excellence* has potential to fulfil the remit of 'democratic schooling' rather better than its predecessors. However, perhaps ominously, the criteria against which school performances in delivery will be judged are unclear. If Inspection reports on school performance continue to deliver a message that academic examination results are the most important aspect of schooling, then this will drive the internal social experiences of the school. It will be clear then, as it is now, that some school students are more equal than others.

It may be that the problems of future democratic schooling are an inevitable consequence of our model of democratic living, as we ride the roller coaster of international capitalism and its greedy consumption of our future through its constant demands that we escalate our consumption in the present. I have argued that we do not have a clear enough map of our present democratic schooling and that before moving forward confidently we should map out rather more fully the territory we are in just now.

However, maybe we do not need a map. As I write, up and down the country, people in school communities are confidently striding forwards to a richer democratic future in schools and schooling, on the back of a positive enthusiasm and some core commitments to democratic values. This is the world of the practitioner, an optimistic 'get on and do' world, occasionally troubled by the tensions which arise from the confused and contradictory conceptual and policy environment in which they work, but seldom allowing that tension to get in the way of their enthusiastic pursuit of what they believe needs to be done. Their optimism, their commitment to young people, their daily struggle to balance freedom and equality in a fair manner, may already set out the best direction into Scotland's democratic future.

Notes

1 These reports, which addressed the curriculum and assessment issues affecting Scottish school pupils aged 14–16, were commissioned by the Scottish Education Department after the Scottish school leaving age was raised to 16 in 1972.
2 See Devine (2000: pp. 91–3) for a brief account of the foundation of the parish schools, though Anderson (1985) and Corr (1990) provide useful correctives to the 'mythic' elements of the parish school story.
3 S6, the sixth year of Scottish secondary schooling, is the only year in which all students, now aged 16 or over, have positively chosen to attend school.
4 Key capacities of the Scottish *Curriculum for Excellence* (Learning and Teaching Scotland, 2011).

5 Responsible citizens, successful learners, active contributors, confident individuals' (Learning and Teaching Scotland, 2011).

Democratic Schooling:
Between Outcomes and Deliberation?

Lejf Moos

Introduction

The concept of social justice and democratic education has changed over years from the idea of equal access to education and the just distribution of educational resources to a contemporary mainstream concept of social justice measured by the outcomes of students' learning. The present accountability trend has been criticised heavily for corrupting schools. This criticism targets the relations in high-stake testing systems between outcomes and economic survival.

However, we need to look more closely into the core of what is tested: schools are well rewarded for being effective by having many students perform in national tests. The tests are constructed to measure as fast and accurately as possible the level of student attainment on a narrow scale of skills or active knowledge.

Schools wish to survive so they teach to the test: teach the subject knowledge that is being measured and the ways tests are constructed. This often means using multiple-choice tests. While this reaction is understandable, it does seem to discount the old wisdom that you not only learn what you are taught, but also from the ways in which you are taught. Therefore our students are acquiring skills in literacy and answering multiple-choice questions and they are also learning to work individually.

There are alternatives to this kind of education that may prepare students to become democratic citizens, innovative and creative workers, communicative human beings and socially skilled, engaged members of communities. In this chapter we shall discuss the current trends of accountability in education and point to the ways in which present trends can be counterbalanced.

The accountability systems—a perspective on education

A number of accountability-logics have been found to be active as a background for thinking and acting in education and schools. They are the structure on which we shall discuss education for social justice and democratic schooling:

- *Market place accountability:* schools are seen as services, where service providers deliver educational products to consumers Core concepts are consumer choice, competition and efficiency.
- *Managerial accountability*: there is a focus on planning, control, standards, top-down management and transparency.
- *Public accountability*: the governance of schools takes place through political processes involving policy makers, parents, students and professionals.
- *Professional accountability*: schools are managed and led according to professional, educational standards and professional ethics.
- *Ethical accountability:* schools are held responsible for producing democratic citizens and their comprehensive and overarching socialisation (Moos, 2010; Moos *et al.*, 2011).

All of these logics seem to be active in any school at any time, but the preferences of logics change over time and in conformity with trends and tendencies in society, in the global society and in politics. The logics emerge from different views and perspectives on society and education from neo-liberalism to public governance and various educational visions.

A major trend: neo-liberal public management

The concept of market-place and managerial accountability seems to occur parallel to the emergence of a special, neo-liberal view of societies in a globalised world, that the German philosopher and sociologist, Jürgen Habermas (2001) has described, using four characteristics:

- An anthropological view of human beings as rational instruments willing and able to make informed decisions and to offer their labour freely in the market place.
- An image of a post-egalitarian society that tolerates social marginalisation, expulsion and exclusion.
- An image of a democracy where citizens are reduced to consumers in a market-society, and where the role of the state is redefined to

that of a service agency for clients and consumers.

- Finally, a view that policy should be aimed at dismantling state regulation.

Those are building bricks for a neo-liberalist view of the world, says Habermas. The last of his four characteristics would seem to challenge the very basis of democracy, and if Habermas is correct there have to be fundamentally new conditions for democracy. As a rule society is seen as being comprised of three basic elements—the state, the market and the civil society. Civil society is regulated by communication and community, morality and ethics, trust and reciprocity between subjects. The market is regulated by money, competition and contracts among consumers, while the state is regulated by political power and rules, the social contract and political discussions between (ideally) equal citizens.

The neo-liberal technologies of governance (Dean, 1999; Peters *et al.*, 2000) as well as education rely heavily on the market as the basis for, and logic of, public management. They are founded on the devolution of management from the state to local levels, to local institutions (in the case of education to self-managing schools), to classrooms (classroom management techniques) and to the individual level (self-managing students).

An important aspect of the ways new public management (NPM) has been developed is the strong tendency to take civil conflicts and grievances to the court of law. If people think their physicians have maltreated them in hospital, they take their complaints to the legal system in order to secure compensation. This also applies to parents who think their child should have performed better and achieved more at school. They then instigate legal action and take the school to court (Lugg *et al.*, 2002).

The neo-liberal NPM is an overarching set of principles that are being played out in very different ways in different countries and national contexts. Two core principles are consistently present: marketisation and managerialism are interdependent and represent very strong trends being imposed on most of the world since the Second World War through the initiatives of the World Bank, the International Monetary Fund and transnational agencies like the OECD and the EU Commission (Moos, 2009). Marketisation means the core values are being made effective: e.g. decentralisation, consumer choice, competition, outcomes, effectiveness, efficiency and comparisons.

Governance presupposes agencies of management, but also requires, and gains, the cooperation of the subjects involved. According to Foucault (1991), this is the defining characteristic of every modern society. Governance derives its legitimacy not from a legal-rational authority but from the rationale of market efficiency.

The concept of human beings is transformed from a notion of autonomous citizens into choosers or consumers of services. So, translated into the school context, parents, and their children, 'consume' 'educational services' through the exercise of choice. 'Freedom of choice' is the overriding good as opposed to active involvement as members of a community discussing and influencing decision-making. This logic—more market less state—then regulates every sphere of life.

The second core accountability of NPM is managerial: as citizens as consumers demand to know what the state and its agencies spend tax-money for, and as many decisions are decentralised from state to local authorities and further on to institutions, the state needed to develop new ways of enacting accountability. It thus invented—or took over from transnational agencies—and implemented a wide range of managerial technologies like very detailed goals, standards and indicators, documentations, quality control instruments and testing.

As mentioned, this accountability trend has very often brought specific ways of teaching, teaching to the test. Because schools and teachers want to survive as institutions and also to give their students what is seen as the best foundation for advancing in education and life, the top exam results, they want to ensure that students perform well and excel in exams and tests (Nichols and Berliner, 2007).

A long-forgotten insight?

Teachers and educational researchers have known for at least half a century that the way in which life in the classroom is arranged, how teaching is delivered and how students' learning is organised, has a profound impact on what is learned. In his seminal study of what he termed the 'hidden curriculum', Philip W. Jackson (1968) showed how students learned to be patient while waiting for teacher to find the time to communicate, to control themselves as members of a large group of peers, to distinguish between work and leisure time activities, to tolerate boredom and so on

– while being taught literacy and other subjects in classrooms in ways that were commonly used in the 1960s in the USA.

Today, classroom observations and analysis show similar results: when students are asked to write assignments, individually, or complete tests, individually, they are getting used to working and thinking individually. This individualistic trend is not only seen in classrooms, because it is a very common, broader societal and cultural trend (Baumann, 1999) which is reinforced in schools.

One of the challenges in teaching classes is to establish and maintain good working, teaching and learning conditions for all students. This seems to always have been a challenge, but it is met with different means, with different social technologies over time and culture. Per Fibæk Laursen (2007) has a very interesting analysis of the ways Danish teachers have tried to maintain good working conditions over time. From the beginning of the nineteen century, and for a hundred years or so, there existed strict rules for good behaviour in classrooms and teachers made students obey them by using corporal punishment and humiliation. From the beginning of the twentieth century a set of new social technologies was developed: classroom discipline. Teachers were given a range of good advice for managing classroom behaviour that would promote good behaviour: looking straight at the student in order to make the student aware that they were being observed, calling out the student's name, and so on. All of those actions took as their point of departure a code of behaviour that the teacher prescribed or that was described in the tradition. For some twenty years now we have witnessed the emergence of a spectrum of classroom management or leadership styles. At one end of the spectrum there is a prolongation of the discipline trends, often named classroom management, and at the other there is a push towards more inclusion, more negotiation and interaction between students and teacher.

There is no doubt that we can find many of these social technologies in contemporary classrooms. Sometimes a technology or approach is chosen because traditions point that way, because educational authorities want teachers to act in special ways and sometimes because teachers choose their own style. All choices are based on diverse basic educational concepts of the educational system: does it see itself as effective, or as more inclusive and collaborative?

It is important not to ignore the effectiveness concept. Being effective in education means focusing on how students individually attain the aims and goals set out in national or local regulations and curriculum, as measured in exams and tests. Many educational systems have written social aims into their curriculum. It can, for example, be education for citizenship, for social responsibility or for communication. However, if those aims are not measured, we know that schools have a tendency not to prioritise them in their daily work.

The analysis of these social technologies could be put into perspective by accountability logic, the professional accountability trend. Professional standards and ethics are developed in an ongoing interplay between teachers' educations and experiences with cultural and political expectations. In some instances we see a strong teacher influence on that interplay, in others the political and cultural influence is stronger. For the time being, it seems that teachers are losing some of their influence and politics and management is taking over and penetrating the practices in classrooms deeply.

Schools and teachers have always made use of social technologies, in some cases they developed them themselves, in other cases they are being injected from the outside. The tightening of the couplings between state authorities and schools through detailed and formalised learning goals and frequent testing seem to work efficiently and effectively in forming practices in schools.

The purpose of education: *Democratic Bildung* and deliberation

All societies need to prepare for the succession of the next generation. They socialise children and youth to be able and willing to take on the values of a given society. This can be described as the sociological explanation for schooling.

There is also a cultural explanation for schooling: many societies and educational systems were built on the understanding that schools were the major cultural institution that sustained societies, because they wanted to ensure that the next generation of citizens were brought up and educated to develop and maintain the society and culture. Thus educational purposes were often described in broad terms: schools should educate students to become enlightened, participating, active and collaborating citizens. *Democratic Bildung* therefore aims to foster maturity, reflexivity, social judgement, aesthetic and political consciousness and competence of action. Basic values in schools are thus social justice, equity, empowerment and community. These notions still live in schools in many places, but are not always furthered by politicians and administrators.

It is a matter of what is traditionally called subject content, and of liberal education, in German: *Bildung*. Children have to learn to become human beings and must, therefore, be educated so that they are able to function independently in their own culture and in the wider society. They cannot live with their parents indefinitely but must eventually leave the childhood home and make a living and have a family of their own.

This ideal does, however, rest on a fundamental paradox. It is one that continues to occupy theorists and practitioners to the present day. How is it possible—through external influence—to bring human beings to a state where they are not controlled by external influences? (Nelson, 1970, in Oettingen, 2001: p. 9)

This perplexing question addressed by educational theorists a century ago is still at the heart of the debate about schooling in a democratic society. We know that young children are not able to take care of themselves. They must be educated. Parents educate children and they leave it to schools and other institutions to educate on their behalf. Education is, inescapably, an external influence. As such, how is it possible to bring about a truly liberating education?

Oettingen (2001) suggests two fundamental principles in resolving the paradox: the *Bildsamkeit* of the child and the request for 'self-reflection'. *Bildsamkeit* refers to a fundamental, innate ability to be open-minded and to participate in a shared praxis. The concept acknowledges the child's 'not-yet-condition'—it has not become what it is going to be—but the child must participate in the educational interaction in order to become fully human:

> 'Self-reflection' means that the self is able to focus its attention on something in the outer world and at the same time on itself. This ability enables the human being to act and to reflect on the action and thereafter initiate other actions. A primary task for teachers is, therefore, to encourage and help children to engage in self-reflection. (Moos, 2003)

This, in short, is how we interpret ethical accountability. Pursuing goals of this kind has been a major concern for many educationalists over an extended period. Besides the opportunity for action, participation and deliberation, we find that the most important concept related to democracy is 'critique' because it gives a more precise direction to the concept of deliberative democracy.

In line with this understanding we find that Beane and Apple (1999) and Furman and Starrat (2002) describe the central concerns of democratic schools as:

- the open flow of ideas, regardless of their popularity, that enables people to be as fully informed as possible;
- the use of critical reflection and analysis to evaluate ideas, problems, and policies;
- the welfare of others and pursuit of the 'common good';
- the concern for the dignity and rights of individuals and minorities.

For Dewey, who has been a great inspiration for many theorists as well as practitioners, democratic leadership meant that democracy was lived through participation in the everyday practice of school life:

> What the argument for democracy implies is that the best way to produce initiative and constructive power is to exercise it. Power, as well as interest, comes by use and practice … The delicate and difficult task of developing character and good judgement in the young needs every stimulus and inspiration possible … I think, that unless democratic habits and thought and action are part of the fibre of a people, political democracy is insecure. It cannot stand in isolation. It must be buttressed by presence of democratic methods in all social relationships. (Dewey, 1937: p. 345)

It is useful to position the view of democracy that is used by Dewey, Beane and Apple and also by the present author: the concept of deliberative democracy, which seems to be the most appropriate and helpful concept with regard to schools and education. Closely linked to the concept of deliberative democracy is the ideal of the 'better argument'.

The rational ideal calls on participants to strive to build communication on the ideal of the better argument that prevails without the use of coercion (Habermas, 1984). This ideal refers to communicative relations among participants that—to the extent possible—seek mutual understanding and aim to minimise the exercise of dominance within institutional relations that must necessarily be asymmetric and embedded within particular organisational structures.

When discussing democratic schooling we need to bear in mind that the interactions in school and also in classrooms take place in organisations. This 'open flow' takes place in groups of people who are only part-time members of the organisations or the communities. Inevitably, they are also members of other communities: their families, peer groups, cultural or political associations and so on. They are carrying different values, norms and interests from one community to the other communities, and at the same time taking different positions in the communities. Sometimes they are leaders, sometimes followers, sometimes children, sometimes parents and so on. Therefore communities in schools will never reach full consensus, but, regardless of the divergences, they need to act. In this situation we find that the position Karen Seashore Louis takes is very productive:

> Many contemporary democratic theorists argue that the most essential element of democratic communities today is their ability to engage in civilized but semi-permanent disagreement. Articulating a humanist voice that calls for respecting and listening to all positions—but then being able to move forward in the absence of consensus—will be the critical skill that school leaders need to develop when the environment makes consensus impossible. (Louis, 2003: p. 105)

Semi-permanent disagreement seems to be at the core of a multicultural, multi-ethnic and multi class community, like schools and their classrooms. The complexity of the community being one cornerstone for the kind of democracy one can hope for. But most important is the ability to progress and move forward. This can only be done with some kind of negotiation where the values and interests are brought to the front and temporarily adjusted to the values and interests of other members.

Communication and interaction

The core of teaching and leading is influencing students and staff. Generally speaking, we can identify three different forms of influence that teachers and school leaders make use of in their daily practice: (1) Direct power is being used when leaders direct, regulate or command followers to do something or not. This can be achieved if the formal and practical position allows for it. (2) Strategic influence is put to use when leaders focus on aspects of practice that need to be changed over time. Strategic planning can often single out a direction that the organisation—school or class—needs to follow, but strategic plans are often not fulfilled because the context changes. (3) Reciprocal influence takes place in interactions, communications and negotiations between leaders and followers. Both parties can set the agenda and table interesting and relevant issues, but of course the leader has more scope for that, being in a formal position to do so (Moos, 2011).

To understand the reciprocal influence better, we find that a communicative model of decision-making is helpful. This model describes decision-making in three phases: construction of premises, decision-making and connection (Moos, 2009).

The phases in this model of influence are very much interconnected and build on each other: decisions are over time developed into social technologies or they form the premises for new decisions. In many cases, connections are also transformed into decisions or naturalised into social technologies. This interconnectedness of phases of influence is one point we wanted to stress in putting them into this single model. Another point is to illustrate that there are many forms of interplay between structural and cultural forms of influences, like finances or discourses, and agent-driven influences, like sense making or direct power. And yet another point to underscore is that influence is often hidden or concealed, but it is still based on decisions made at one point and by somebody.

Constructing premises

In the first phase of processes of decision-making, influence is present because of the way *premises* are defined or produced, and by whom. Who (individuals, groups, institutions) defines the situation or the problem at hand? How is the dominant discourse on which decisions and actions are based created, or how is 'the definition of reality' constructed?

It is important to distinguish between agent-driven and structural influences. There are a number of ways that individual agents or groups can influence the minds and interpretations of other agents. They can set an agenda, influence sense making and set the stage, and enter into educational activities, negotiations or other interactions.

Another form of power is the discourse. The concept of discourse indicates that discussions of relations and influence are not 'natural', but are, instead, constructed over time as a result of struggles between stakeholders. The constructive effect of these influences is the focus of this category, which covers setting the scene or stage for decision-making. The actions themselves (setting the agenda, sense making, and engaging in discourses) are not seen as decisions, but as foundations for decision-making. However, the ingredients for the process of construction are the results of selections. These ingredients can be the agents' selection of topics and ways of sense making, the institutions'—in a very broad sense—selection of foci for dominant discourses, and the selections made in complex organisations through processes of emergence beyond the control of individuals.

Decision-making

This is a complicated procedure involving the selection of accepted and sufficiently important premises that are influential enough to be taken into account. Decisions can be made by individual or collectives of agents, and are often called 'direct power'. Decisions can also result in a new agenda for discussing or making decisions about the field, or for the description and regulation of new behaviours.

Decisions are often built into structures: legislation, societal, social and financial frames. Institutions are constructed because of political processes and power struggles that have sanctions attached to them. The agents' forms of direct power also have the possibility of sanctions being attached to them. However, none of these forms can guarantee results unless they are viewed—or even identified—as legitimate forms by the people and groups affected by them. On the other hand, decisions construct the premises for new decisions. This construction is the case with leadership decisions that form the premises for employer decisions.

As mentioned above, the transnational agencies have no or little legal power to make decisions on behalf of the national governments.

Connection phase

The third major phase of influence is the connection phase. Inspired by communication theories, a communication is only viewed as an effective communication if it 'irritates' the other pole to such a degree that it chooses to connect, to stop and reflect on, and possibly alter, their reflection process and practice. Whether or not the other agent is connecting can be difficult to detect since some reactions might occur long after the 'irritation' has taken place. On the other hand, there is no point in talking about influence without effects. If the act of law does not change anything concerning citizen behaviour, or if army privates do not follow a colonel's orders, then we cannot talk about a real influence. The ways in which connections are made become an important feature of the construction of premises for future decisions.

Today, we see a whole range of technologies of performance: developing budgets, performance indicators, benchmarking, audits, accountability, tests, ranking. The broad field of evaluation and assessment is currently undergoing basic transformations. National as well as local systems and organisations need documentation for the use of resources in the organisations in their jurisdiction. An important aspect of the hunt for transparency involves finding out to whom agents and organisations should be accountable, and which values they should be accountable for. Schools must answer to a range of different accountabilities, for example, a market-place accountability that focuses on efficiency and competition, a bureaucratic accountability that focuses on outcomes and indicators, a political accountability that focuses on citizen satisfaction and negotiations, a professional accountability that focuses on professional expertise and an ethical accountability that focuses on social justice. Schools must simultaneously answer to all of these accountabilities, consequently creating numerous dilemmas for schools and school leaders (Moos et al., 2011).

Deliberative democracy

Following the argument made in the former sections, communicative competencies are pivotal for students as well as citizens of contemporary societies: those are the competencies needed for influencing the construction of premises for decision-making. Community members need to be able to negotiate their positions, their interests and also the meaning of what is going on, or what they think should be going on. Interpretation of impressions and experiences seems to be more important now than ever before because the quantity of information, data and impressions is so very large today. Very often it is impossible for individuals to form interpretations. They need to communicate and negotiate with peers and other people.

Some children are raised in families, where communication skills are developed on a daily basis because parents talk with their children and encourage them to speak up and make their arguments. This makes it easier for them to manage the conversations and dialogues in school and thus to prosper from the community of peers and teachers.

Unfortunately, some children are not that privileged. Their families are not able to or willing to involve them in conversations or deliberations. They cannot provide an appropriate background for an upbringing that encourages participation in democratic conversations and negotiations. So those children are underprivileged and not being brought up to live as independent adults.

Schools in democratic societies therefore have many responsibilities: not only to support children to acquire basic skills and active knowledge that high-stake accountability systems are focusing on, but also to support them in developing good communication competencies.

Another forgotten insight

Experiences from school practices (Moos and Kofod, 2011) show that teaching can be whole-class teaching with the many possibilities for teacher control and student negotiations. In more contemporary teaching forms, like project work and group work, some of the couplings are loosened. The teachers still decide the overarching issue, but students or groups of students can choose the specific problem they want to investigate. The students also choose how to work, how to find solutions to their problems and how to present them to their peers. The teacher sets the practical frames and demands collaboration and product. Those forms are parallel to some of the forms used at the school and team level and therefore there is room for student negotiations in some phases of the work. The negotiations can develop their communicative competencies.

There can be a tradition for open relations between teachers and students in some schools. There can also be traditions for delivering a great deal of instruction verbally: teachers often enter into dialogues, problem-solving processes or discussions with students in class on the basis of circular questioning, thus giving room for student involvement and verbal communication. It is also a tradition that teachers involve students in decisions on what and how they should learn.

The processes of teaching and learning are as important as the actual content of lessons, but these are not measured by managerial accountability regimes.

Part II
Teaching Controversial Issues

Introduction to Part II: Teaching Controversial Issues

> Democratic values and skills are not genetic, they are learned, and in a democracy young people need to develop the abilities to analyse and discuss controversial issues in a peaceful manner based on mutual respect ... what is learned in formal educational settings such as schools is crucial in the development of democratic behaviour. (Chikoko *et al.*, 2011: p. 6)

Grappling with controversial issues teaching is at the very heart of citizenship and democracy, and in promoting an understanding of democratic principles and behaviour. Some would argue that this is the case particularly where addressing controversial issues is seen as fundamental to educating for 'global citizenship', with its emphases on negotiating difference. As one would expect, controversial issues teaching invariably raises challenging and difficult questions that can often prompt emotional responses and difficult feelings.

This themed section illustrates the complexity of teaching controversial issues from three differing standpoints. Hahn, drawing on examples from England, Germany, Denmark and the United States, addresses how our comprehension of the topic is enhanced by evaluating cross-cultural perspectives. Investigating what happens in schools in a range of national settings is illuminating because it can help us re-evaluate and re-think our own deeply held assumptions about what constitutes a controversial issue.

Consequently, such an approach enriches and extends our understanding of controversial issues teaching. Hahn also raises questions about the desirability of impartiality and whether teachers can and should be 'neutral'.

The second contribution is from a teacher educator and lecturer working in Higher Education in Scotland. Britton provides a reflective account of the dilemmas and potential challenges facing training teachers by drawing on a range of perspectives and roles. Interestingly, he discusses his own experience as a pupil and political socialisation during his schooling in Scotland, in addition to his work in the Initial Teacher Education (ITE) field. Britton's main point is that if a prime goal of citizenship education is to encourage assertive and critical citizenry then we need a teaching force that is both comfortable and prepared to teach controversial issues to assertive and active young citizens.

In conclusion to this section, Verma's chapter provides a case study of her practice in New York as a teacher working with Sikh youth in the post- 9/11 context. She shows how racism and stereotypical assumptions were heightened by the subsequent war on terror. She powerfully illustrates how injustice and racism impacts on students' self- confidence and esteem. Significantly, she argues that the way young people learn about other individuals, cultures and experiences that are so very different from their own is fundamental to the purposes of global citizenship. In short, she maintains that this educational process can help navigate the divide between local and global citizenship identities.

What the following chapters clearly demonstrate is that teaching controversial issues can certainly be a testing enterprise, requiring a high level of skill and commitment.

Key questions for this theme include:

- In what ways do controversial issues teaching inform an understanding of democratic principles?
- Are all sensitive issues controversial?
- What can young people and teachers learn from engaging with controversial issues?

The Citizenship Teacher and Teaching Controversial Issues: A Comparative Perspective

Carole L. Hahn

The citizenship teacher and teaching controversial issues

Controversial issues teaching and learning is at the heart of education for citizenship in a democracy. Ever since I was a student in a teacher preparation programme, I have been committed to that principle. In subsequent years, my commitment has deepened, yet I have also come to appreciate how difficult it is to ensure high quality controversial issues teaching for all students. In this chapter, I discuss controversial issues teaching from a comparative perspective, with attention to policy, research and practice in varied countries, including the United States, the United Kingdom and selected European and other countries.

Rationales and policies over time

In the United States there is a long tradition advocating controversial issues teaching in social studies, the part of the curriculum that carries a special responsibility for educating democratic citizens. Progressives such as John Dewey (1916 / 1944) and his followers argued that students are most likely to acquire the knowledge, skills and attitudes needed by citizens of a democracy if they experience democratic processes in their schools, such as deliberation and decision-making about contested issues. Over the years, Alan Griffin (1942 / 1992), Hunt and Metcalf (1955 / 1968), Oliver and Shaver (1966), Newmann and Oliver (1970), Engle and Ochoa (1988), Parker (1996), Evans and Saxe (1996) and Hess (2009) all argued that in a democracy students ought to have the opportunity to investigate and discuss the important, unresolved, controversial issues in society; they ought to read, hear and express diverse views to engage in democratic discourse.

Further, the National Council for the Social Studies (NCSS), the professional association for social studies educators in the United States, has continually asserted the importance to democracy of teachers and students having 'the freedom to teach and to learn' (NCSS, 1977), particularly with respect to controversial issues. For example, the NCSS recommended that:

> It is the explicit policy of the nation's public schools to encourage and maintain the study of the unsolved problems and the current, controversial issues of our society. Only through this study can children develop the abilities they will need as citizens of a democracy—to analyze a problem, to gather and organise facts, to discriminate between fact and opinion, to draw intelligent conclusions, and to accept the principle of majority rule with due respect to minorities. (NCSS, 1977)

In the 1970s and 1980s in response to several conservative attacks against curriculum materials, NCSS leaders asserted the importance of teachers being able to teach controversial issues and students being able to study such issues (Ochoa, 1979; Hahn, 1984). In recent years, the NCSS has continued to reaffirm in official policy statements that: 'students need to learn how to study controversial issues by gathering [information] ... and discussing different viewpoints in order to ... make, clear informed decisions' (NCSS, 2007).

Yet, despite years of advocacy by social studies scholars, leaders of professional associations and some state policymakers, there have been obstacles to turning ideals into widespread practice. Many teachers avoid controversial issues because they do not want to 'make waves' and face criticism by some parents. They fear that they will become the targets of attacks by groups that seek to censor particular topics from the schools. In recent years, the self-censorship of teachers has been compounded by the drive to 'cover' the content stipulated in state curriculum standards (Nelson and Hahn, 2010). Many school and district policy makers emphasise the importance of covering the standards so that students will perform well on state tests that assess knowledge of that content. Some social studies teachers continue to practise 'ambitious teaching' (Grant and Salinas, 2008), going beyond the standards to teach for thoughtfulness, in-depth understanding and deliberation about controversial issues, but they are increasingly rare. In the current climate of high-stakes testing and a focus on literacy and numeracy at the expense of other subjects (Duncan, 2011), there is increased need in the United States to draw attention to the need for controversial issues teaching.

Citizenship educators in the United States are not alone in their interest in controversial issues teaching. In the United Kingdom in the 1970s, the political literacy movement promoted developing students' political literacy through an issues-centred approach (Crick and Heater, 1977; Crick and Porter, 1978). The Humanities Curriculum Project, under the direction of Lawrence Stenhouse, developed curriculum units on the principle that secondary students should investigate and discuss controversial issues (Ruddock, 1983). In the 1980s Robert Stradling wrote a useful book for teachers on how to teach controversial issues. At the first international conferences I attended in 1981 and 1982, Scottish participants reported on the important work being done in teaching controversial issues in the course Modern Studies. In the 1990s, Professor Alex Porter, who had been active in the political literacy movement, was brought back into service to write the section of the Crick Report on controversial issues teaching (Advisory Group on Citizenship, 1998). The summary to that section emphasised: 'While we do not underestimate the difficulties, it is our strong belief that offering pupils the experience of a genuinely free consideration of difficult issues forms a vital and worthwhile part of citizenship education' (Advisory Group on Citizenship, 1998: p. 60).

More recently, Maitles (2005) recommended the teaching of controversial issues in Scotland, referring to a case study of a primary school in the West of Scotland in which children successfully studied the war in Iraq. Additionally, Claire and Holden (2007) edited a volume of case studies of controversial issues teaching in varied sites in the United Kingdom, as well as in several other countries. Authors described projects using children's literature, drama and history to teach children in the UK about war and peace, climate change, and development aid. Other authors describe a variety of teaching methods for teaching controversial issues used in classrooms in Canada, Russia, Germany, Japan and South Africa.

Beyond the United States and the United Kingdom, civic educators incorporate controversial issues teaching. For example, Danish social science teachers have a cultural tradition that emphasises democratic teaching, including controversial issues teaching. The law says that the *folkskole* (for students ages 5–16) should model democracy, which is assumed to include the discussion of controversial issues. Teachers who participated in the 1968 student movements internalised values that were reflected in laws requiring them to present multiple sides of contentious issues to students. Today, the younger generation of Danish social science teachers I have met continue to value the spirit in national policies that asserts the importance of exploring diverse views on controversial issues.

The political educators who I first met in the 1980s in Germany were deeply committed to controversial issues teaching as a reflection of their own historical experience and contemporary discourse. In the years following the Second World War, many political educators helped to write new curriculum and implement policies to promote the discussion of controversial issues as an essential part of the democratisation of education. Like the Danish teachers, many of the German teachers and teacher educators working in the area of political education were activists in the 1968 youth movement. Additionally, Habermas' ideas had influenced the thinking of young scholars of the day who were writing curriculum materials. There was widespread support for *Lander*-level policies that required the teaching of diverse views on controversial issues.

These are just a few examples of the rationales and policies for controversial issues teaching that have been prevalent in several different Western democracies for decades. Next, I turn to some of the empirical research from different national contexts that focus on varied aspects of controversial issues teaching and learning.

Research

There are three distinct, yet overlapping, features of controversial issues teaching that are evident in the research: content, pedagogy and climate (Hahn, 1996a). Controversial or conflictual content focuses on historic or contemporary issues over which citizens disagree. Topics that may be controversial in one community or country may not be controversial in another. Moreover, controversies shift in time. Hess (2009) refers to a 'tipping point' when controversial issues move from open (unresolved, not an agreed right answer) to closed (there is a widely accepted right answer). Controversial issues content is a necessary, but not sufficient condition, for controversial issues teaching. The use of conflictual pedagogy and an open, supportive classroom climate for discussion are equally important. Conflictual pedagogy is the process a teacher uses to enable students to confront differing views on an issue. This may include having students analyse newspaper articles, policy options or video clips in which authors or speakers argue differing sides of issues. Students may engage in a debate, participate in a deliberative discussion or write a policy paper in which they consider alternative positions.

Bickmore (1991) studied the classes of four teachers who used varied amounts of conflictual content and pedagogy and found that in the class that used the most controversial issues content and pedagogy, the course was complex and challenging—both for the students to learn and the teacher to teach. Although students often engaged in decision-making about issues and seemed stimulated by the dialogue, not every student responded positively. Hess (2009) conducted a series of case studies of exemplary controversial political issues (CPI) teachers. She found that effective CPI teachers plan carefully for controversial issues discussions. They teach students how to discuss and they expect students to enter the discussions having read the necessary background material that presents diverse views. Additionally, Hess (2009) identified varied ways that skilled teachers bring out the ideological diversity in a classroom—even when that diversity is not initially apparent.

The third element of controversial issues teaching is an 'open classroom climate' in which students agree to statements such as 'my teacher respects our opinions and encourages us to express them', 'in our classes we often discuss controversial political, economic, and social issues', 'in our classes our teachers present more than one side on an issue', 'we are encouraged to consider many points of view on issues', and 'students feel free to express opinions in class, even when their opinions are different from the teacher or other students' (Ehman, 1969; Hahn, 1998; Torney-Purta et al., 2001). Researchers have focused specifically on 'classroom climate' more than other dimensions of controversial issues teaching, although controversial issues content and pedagogy are presumed to be present when students report that there is an open, supportive climate for discussion.

Various researchers have found that when students in the United States reported that their classes were characterised by an open climate, the students reported higher levels of political interest, political efficacy, political trust and a sense of civic duty than did comparable samples who experienced a less open climate (Ehman, 1969; 1970; Baughman 1975; Blankenship, 1990. For a review of this early research cf. Hahn, 1998, chapter 5). In a recent longitudinal study, researchers found that students who reported debating issues in school were more likely in later years to be engaged politically and civically; they were more likely to follow news most of the time, to be involved in organisations outside of school, to raise money for charities, to sign petitions, to participate in boycotts and to attend community meetings (Zukin *et al.*, 2006). Additionally, researchers in the United States have found that controversial issues discussion in an open, supportive classroom climate is especially important for Latino and African-American students from low-income backgrounds to develop political interest and efficacy, a commitment to civic participation and expectations of voting when they are adults (Ehman, 1970; Torney-Purta *et al.*, 2007; Kahne and Sporte, 2008). Other researchers have explored some of the subtle effects of controversial issues discussions with diverse populations of students and with the development of 'political tolerance' or a willingness to extend rights to diverse groups (Hess and Avery, 2008).

In my study of controversial issues teaching in Denmark, England, Germany, the Netherlands and the United States, I obtained similar findings both within and across countries. When students said they had an opportunity to discuss controversial issues in an open classroom climate, they were more likely to have higher levels of political interest, efficacy, trust, and confidence than students without such experiences (Hahn, 1998).

In recent years, researchers studying samples of students in several other national contexts also found a positive correlation between controversial issues discussion and student civic interest and engagement. For example, in Israel researchers found that students who perceived an open climate for discussion in their civics classes reported higher levels of political efficacy, political participation and democratic orientations than did students without an open climate (Perlinger *et al.*, 2006). In Ukraine, partner organisations in Poland and the United States worked with

Ukrainian civic educators to develop a new curriculum and to prepare teachers to use democratic pedagogy. The evaluators of the curriculum found that project students were more likely to say that teachers presented several sides of issues and encouraged students to express their views than did comparison group students who did not participate in the programme (Craddock, 2005). Additionally, students in the treatment group were more likely to be supportive of rights for immigrants and for women than those in the control group, and they were more likely to score higher on a test of civic knowledge.

In a recent study, another non-governmental organisation in the United States has partnered with civic educators in Azerbaijan, the Czech Republic and Lithuania to develop curriculum materials and train teachers to use a pedagogical approach to discuss controversial issues (Avery and Simmons, 2008). They reported that teachers and students found the project's model easy to use and the students enjoyed having discussions about controversial issues. The students also reported that they learned about the issues, discussed national and international issues with their teachers more than they had previously, and liked hearing diverse views and being encouraged to express their own views.

These studies of samples of students in different countries are insightful. However, the largest and most comprehensive studies that looked at classroom climate for discussion were the Civic Education Study of the International Association for the Evaluation of Educational Achievement, better known as the IEA CIVED Study and the recent International Civic and Citizenship Study (ICCS) of IEA (Torney-Purta *et al.*, 2001; Schulz *et al.*, 2010). In the 28-nation study of representative samples of 14-year olds in 28 countries in 1999 (n = 90,000), the CIVED researchers used a regression analysis to identify a number of variables that predicted student civic knowledge and students' expectations of voting in the future as adults. The researchers found that an open classroom climate was a predictor of civic knowledge for samples in 22 countries and of expected voting in 20 countries. Interestingly, female students in 23 out of the 28 countries reported that the classroom climate was more open than did the male students. A similar gender difference was found in other studies (Hahn, 1996b; 1998; 2010). Looking at student responses to particular items on the Classroom Climate scale among samples from Australia, Hong Kong and the United

States, a similar pattern emerged in the three countries: students were more likely to agree that they were encouraged to express their views and to say that they felt comfortable doing so than to report that in their classes they discussed issues about which people disagree—controversial issues (Hahn, 2010). The ICCS data set will soon be available for researchers to conduct secondary analyses, including exploring relationships between Classroom Climate and other variables.

Practice

In my observations of classrooms in four European countries and the United States I have noticed distinct pedagogical approaches to the handling of controversial issues (Hahn, 1998). For example, in England, I have often observed discussions of ethical issues in lessons in 'personal, social, and health education' and 'religious education/studies'. I have seen students express their views in small groups sitting around a table on what they believe is right or wrong with respect to abortion, fox hunting, women priests, equal opportunities and gender discrimination and other issues (Hahn, 1998). Recently, I observed students in 'citizenship' lessons in one urban school expressing their views on school policies, such as privacy issues related to a student identification card, as well as on international issues, such as nuclear non-proliferation.

In Germany, I have frequently observed students sitting at desks arranged in a large horseshoe shape carrying on a whole-class *Pro–Contra* (for–against) discussion of a public policy issue (Hahn, 1998). Topics included whether the laws should be changed dealing with the age for voting in *Lander*-level elections, the right of asylum and citizenship. In 'social studies' and 'social science' classes, students frequently discuss differing views as presented in newspaper and magazine articles and on editorial pages about current issues. In those subjects as well as in history lessons, students are often presented with differing theoretical positions on topics. Danish students also investigate differing theoretical positions when they study topics from sociology, economics, political science and international relations in their social science classes (Hahn, 1998).

Danish students are required to conduct independent research projects and many of them focus on controversial policy issues. For example, in 2010 at one gymnasium (upper secondary school) students told me about their research projects on policies related to climate change, the obesity epidemic and Muslims in Denmark.

In the United States, a typical practice in social studies classes is a teacher-led discussion of current events in the news. Many students are also expected to 'do a term paper' (independent research project) on a contemporary issue, such as capital punishment, gun control or health care (Hahn, 1998). Unfortunately, in recent years the emphasis on covering content so that students can do well on state tests seems to have reduced the attention to controversial issues teaching. However, some teachers remain committed to preparing their students to engage with difficult controversial issues. At the annual meeting of the National Council for the Social Studies in 2010, delegates to the NCSS House of Delegates unanimously passed a resolution that said in part:

> Whereas controversy, discourse, debate, compromise and differences of opinions and values are all part of the democratic experience; whereas the world beyond the classroom confronts all citizens with controversial issues and opinions that some might find objectionable; whereas the social studies classroom is an appropriate environment for the consideration of differing points of view; be it resolved as common state standards for social studies are developed, NCSS would continue to support social studies standards that challenge students to explore a range of points of view when considering historical interpretations and contemporary issues ... (NCSS, 2011: p. 168)

Importantly, Hess (2009) found that exemplary CPI teachers carefully plan for controversial issues discussions, using a variety of methods to scaffold the discussion. Hess (2010) does not recommend leading such discussions spontaneously, when neither the teacher nor the students have done careful preparation before the discussion begins. The exemplary CPI teachers Hess (2009) studied expect students to come to class having completed background reading and prepared for their participation. They teach students to listen carefully, treat each other with respect and cite evidence to support their views. The teacher's role as a facilitator of discussion includes asking students to elaborate on a point to deepen student thinking (probing); at other times, to broaden student participation, the teacher asks students if they agree, disagree or have another view (redirecting). The teachers welcome student comments, as their goal is to create and sustain a classroom climate in which students feel comfortable expressing their views and in which all students learn. Effective CPI teachers' careful planning for controversial issues discussions reflects the three dimensions of content, pedagogy and climate. They focus on issues content that is appropriate to their subject and their students. And they continually work to ensure an open, supportive climate.

Teachers use a variety of pedagogical models to scaffold student discussions. I will elaborate on four widely used models here and then mention several curriculum projects that use other pedagogical approaches. Parker (2006) has written extensively about the first two models—seminars and deliberations. Seminars focus on seeking understanding whereas deliberations emphasise making decisions about public issues. In a seminar, the teacher and students discuss the meaning of a text, working together to listen and learn from one another as they seek enhanced understanding. A class might use a seminar format to understand an editorial about a controversial issue, such as a proposed new immigration policy. In a deliberation, students think out loud in a discussion as together they decide a course of action to address an identified problem, be it a school policy or a national or international policy. The class that held a seminar discussion one day on differing positions on immigration policies might the next day have a deliberation discussion to answer the question: What should be our country's policy on immigration?

One model that contains the elements of both a seminar and a deliberation is a value analysis or value inquiry model. Although different authors proposed variations on this model, the one proposed by Banks *et al.* (1999) is typical of this approach. After reading a text or viewing a video, the teacher leads the whole class through a series of questions, or gives students a discussion guide for small-group discussion that follows a sequence of questions: What is the problem here? Who has done or said what? What might they value that influences their position? What are the alternative positions that are possible? What might or could happen if each alternative policy is followed? What do you think should be done, and why? What does that show that you value?

A fourth format for discussion is called 'structured academic controversy' (SAC). The model grew out of research by Johnson and Johnson at the University of Minnesota that focused on the benefits of cooperative learning and the role of conflict in enhancing student learning (Avery and Simmons, 2008). Students are given a set of prepared materials containing arguments for two different positions on a controversial public policy issue. In groups of four students, first, two students present one view while the other two students listen, then ask questions to clarify points. In the second stage, the other two students present their position, followed by questions and answers for clarification. In the third stage, the students switch roles and present the opposite view to what they originally presented. Finally, the group of four students deliberate about what they think the best position would be, trying to reach consensus on a policy, which might be different from or adaptations of either of the two positions originally presented. Civic educators in a number of Eastern European countries and the United States have successfully used a curriculum based on this approach—*Deliberating Democracy*, supported by the Constitutional Rights Foundation in Chicago (see www.deliberating.org). As I noted earlier, both the teachers and the students who participated in the project found the model easy to use; the students also reported learning more about issues than they had previously and liking the approach (Avery and Simmons, 2008).

Several other curriculum projects based in the United States use differing models to structure investigation into and discussion of controversial issues. The National Issues Forum, developed by the Kettering Foundation, focuses on a set of public policy alternatives to national policies, such as health care or immigration reform. The Choices for the 21st Century Project, based at Brown University, focuses on alternatives to foreign policy issues, such as: what should be the US policy in Afghanistan? (see www.choices.edu). Further, a 'public issues model' developed by the staff of the Harvard Social Studies Project (Oliver and Shaver 1966; Newmann and Oliver 1970) has been adapted and widely used to explore diverse controversial issues (Singleton 1996; Hess 2009;and see www.soc-sci-ed-consortium.org/publications.html).

Clearly, there is no one model of 'best practice' for controversial issues teaching. The important point is that teachers should carefully select a model to scaffold students' investigations and discussions of controversial issues. What is effective in one class may not be as effective in another class-room or national context. Nevertheless, by attending to content, pedagogy and climate, teachers can enhance student learning of controversial issues.

Summary

Looking at policy, research and practice in differing democratic societies, the complexity and importance of controversial issues teaching is evident. Importantly, by looking beyond one's own national context, educators can gain insights to previously taken-for-granted assumptions and see with fresh eyes how to enhance education for democratic citizenship in the future.

The Citizenship Teacher and Controversial Issues

Alan Britton

Introduction

This chapter provides a critical reflection on the relationship between the citizenship teacher and controversial issues. In doing so it highlights the ways in which the 'citizenship teacher' (whether designated as a subject specialist, or as a generalist practitioner) has the potential to foster an understanding of controversy among young people. It will examine the ways in which the effective navigation and mediation of controversial issues can present opportunities for enhancing capacity for critical and active citizenship. It begins with a brief analysis of two critical incidents from my own experience as a pupil and then as a tutor that are intended to help the framing of some core issues. I then define what I mean by the notion of controversy and controversial issues. Thereafter I offer a series of related observations and recommendations for pedagogy and practice that are of relevance to the effective teaching of controversial issues in the context of citizenship education.

My contribution is derived from a practice perspective, and is rooted in the Scottish educational context with which I am most familiar, although I hope that the conclusions are sufficiently relevant and universal as to be of interest to a wider readership. What do I mean by a 'practice perspective', and why does the practice perspective matter? While there are undoubtedly key philosophical and epistemological considerations of relevance to the teaching of controversial issues, we ought also to be 'enquiring into matters of contextual detail, and in particular into what is actually happening in classrooms' (McLaughlin, 2003: p. 149). Indeed particular concerns about the efficacy and impact of a great deal of classroom practice in this area are sometimes raised, including this somewhat blunt assessment:

'Teaching controversial issues, particularly those of a socio-scientific nature, has never been easy or particularly successful—all too often students contribute little to the discussion' (Levinson, 2006: p1218).

Some official evaluation of school effectiveness around controversial issues has echoed this rather negative view, noting that provision [in this instance in the English context] was: 'inadequate where teachers' subject knowledge was insufficient for them to deal with sensitive and controversial issues or where there was insufficient emphasis on these in the curriculum' (Ofsted, 2010: p. 7).

Such concerns are not solely a contemporary phenomenon, and it is significant to note the list of issues that one author identified as potential sources of controversy for a teacher in the context of early 1950s America: 'Among the problems I shall face as a social studies teacher are sex education, evolution, segregation, socialism, communism, pacificism [sic], and taxation, to mention only a few' (Cline, 1953: p. 337).

While there is a fairly well-established critical literature (of broadly negative and positive dispositions alike) on the issue of controversial issues in the classroom, it seems timely to review issues of practice in this area, given the widespread resurgence in interest in citizenship education across many educational systems. The policy relevance of such a review is thus reinforced in the light of a number of related contemporary developments across the globe, including widespread trends of curriculum change that favour the promotion of 'citizenship', alongside topical reviews of the nature and standards of teacher professionalism (for a recent example in Scotland, cf. Donaldson, 2011; and in England, Coates, 2011).

In short, there is an expectation in many countries that teachers (whether specialists or not) should be ready and willing to address elements of a citizenship 'curriculum' that are likely to stray into controversial territory; and at the same time the frameworks and definitions of teacher professionalism place ever greater demands with regard to the skill set, craft and nimbleness of the teacher in navigating such terrain.

It is hoped that my own personal and professional biography that I draw upon here can offer some reflexive insights from a range of perspectives and roles. I refer below to a formative experience as a school pupil. My subsequent understanding of these issues has been moulded by time served as a secondary level teacher of languages (not especially controversial) and Modern Studies (a Scottish curricular peculiarity focusing on elements of politics, sociology and economics that, as will be seen, has considerable *potential* to be controversial).

Later in my career I worked at the Scottish Parliament in a non-partisan educational capacity where strict neutrality was a fundamental professional requirement, enshrined in a code of conduct. Most recently in my capacity as a teacher educator and university tutor, thanks to the principle of academic freedom I have greater scope for controversy yet I sometimes feel a vestigial nagging pull of neutrality from earlier in my career that occasionally impacts on aspects of my pedagogy and professional identity. Colleagues who emerged from a different pathway of professional formation will perhaps feel less inhibited!

There is an apparent peculiarity of the Scottish context that ought to be noted here for the benefit of non-native readers. To many outside observers, the Scottish educational system appears to function from the basis of a broad operational consensus that is regarded with envy by some and that appears to render most aspects of policy and practice largely uncontroversial and uncontested in themselves. Scottish education does not appear to be subject to the upheavals found elsewhere of shifting ideology or political influences. To others this picture would, however, be misleading, and in their view the reality is that educational controversy and dissent is present but is often sidelined or marginalised. It has earned the dubious status of 'received wisdom' (Humes, 1986: p. 6), and a 'story' or 'myth' (Humes and Bryce, 2008: p. 99).

I raise this issue here because it has implications for one of my underpinning arguments: that if one of the authentic goals of citizenship education is the formation of a more assertive and challenging citizenry, and if we are serious about the effective teaching of controversial issues, we require a teaching force which is itself comfortable with challenging and sensitive topics. Both the citizen-in-formation (the pupil or student) and teacher-as-citizen have to understand and engage with *controversy* as a phenomenological and epistemological concept; that is, it ought to involve engagement with matters of experience, perception and evidential truth. One consequence of this might manifest itself in a teaching profession that is more willing to challenge consensus and the 'received wisdom' described above.

I will now highlight two critical incidents (Tripp, 1993), drawn from my own experiences as both pupil and teacher, that have helped to shape my own stance. Tripp characterises such an approach as being 'critical of everything except being critical' (Tripp, 1998: p. 37), which resonates with any attempt to address controversiality. I will then offer a number of observations and recommendations that might help to frame and delineate the professional capacity required for the teaching of controversial issues, whether in the Scottish context or elsewhere.

Setting the scene: two critical incidents

I have chosen two critical incidents on my personal and professional learning journey that, while constituting subjective accounts, have been especially persuasive influences on my view of controversial issues, one pertaining to my experience as a pupil, the other as a teacher educator. Such incidents are by their nature subjective yet they have some merit in crystallising a particular issue and acting as an aid to problem solving, professional judgement and decision-making (cf. Bell, 2005: pp. 178–82 for an extended discussion of such methodologies).

The first incident dates from my time as a secondary school pupil in the early-mid 1980s. Some pupils became aware that one of our teachers had been the subject of a complaint from a parent alleging that he was seeking to indoctrinate the pupils in his care. The teacher in question certainly made no secret of his own political and ideological allegiances. One of his more innovative contributions to the extra-curricular life of some pupils including myself was to offer lifts in his car to Miners' rallies (this was at the time of the UK Miners' Strike[1]). Was I thus (along with classmates) a victim of indoctrination? According to Cohen (1969: p. 180), the indoctrinating teacher:

> can be identified whenever one of a number of points of view is presented as though it were the only one possible; whenever questions are suppressed rather than answered; whenever certain areas of questioning are taboo; and whenever the educator is psychologically unable to tolerate the expression of dissenting views.

My recollection of this teacher's classroom practice is that different shades of opinion and ideology were in fact considered and respected. Equally significantly, this teacher inspired me to go on to study politics at university. My conclusion with the benefit of hindsight is that his intention was to politicise, yes, but not to indoctrinate: an important distinction that the aspiring teacher of citizenship might reflect on. In my subsequent career as a teacher in the same subject area I was much more cautious in my approach, perhaps at the expense of failing directly to inspire and promote a political awakening among my own pupils.

A much more recent relevant incident arose when I visited a school to observe an undergraduate teaching student deliver a lesson during her third-year placement. She was teaching a Primary 7 class (age group approximately 11 years old) about climate change. During the lesson she used as a visual aid a very striking photograph of a polar bear looking forlorn and isolated on a melting ice floe. The children's spontaneous response was an audible and very heartfelt cry of sympathy and concern. For the sake of balance should the conscientious teacher immediately reassure the children that polar bears can in fact swim for at least fifty miles across the open sea in order to reach new hunting grounds?

This incident appears to be a *prima facie* case of a (student) teacher manipulating the pupils' opinions and world view, whether consciously or unconsciously. In this case, and around this topic, is the apparent bias somehow more acceptable due to conformity with the wider prevailing scientific and curricular orthodoxy? Frank Furedi, who represents a particular strain of left-leaning yet strongly libertarian and sceptical thinking in current intellectual discourse in the UK, maintains that the promotion of potentially emotive resources and perspectives reduces education to a form of 'reverse socialisation', exploiting the pester power of young people to target parental attitudes and behaviours. He further suggests that: 'preying on children's fears and exploiting their anxiety is now considered to be a form of enlightened education' (Furedi, 2009).

In posing these questions and airing these concerns I am not seeking to associate myself with a particular ideological position or with those who would deny the nature of climate change; rather my concern lies in the areas of epistemology and critical thinking that in turn ought to lie at the heart of the pedagogy of controversial issues.

Such concerns around controversial issues and the wider role of citizenship education are not restricted to any one point on the political spectrum. It is an area that is maligned by left and right alike. On the left there are those who see citizenship education as a cynical mechanism to promote passive conformity and to exert control (for example, Gillborn, 2006: p. 95; Pykett, 2007), as a subtle reinforcement of middle-class social, political and economic predominance (Reay, 2008), or the perpetuator of forms of discrimination such as institutionalised racism (Gillborn, 2006).

It is also unappreciated by some on the right, where the distinction between traditional approaches and more recent developments (which are apparently inherently biased) is emphasised:

> Modern citizenship lessons have little in common with tra-
> ditional, factual 'civics' and a glance at the teaching materials
> shows that the subject has a leftish, 'progressive' bias. Some
> common sense is intermingled with a great deal of ideological
> nonsense, making the two difficult to separate. But that does not
> mean the teaching is acceptable. (Campaign for Real Education,
> 2006)

More explicitly pedagogical objections to citizenship education and its apparent preferred methodologies are also a concern on the Right:

> Education for Citizenship is disingenuous in many respects.
> Given full information, and choice, parents would be unlikely
> to welcome citizenship or the use of psychological techniques
> such as 'circle time' and 'values clarification' in pursuit of politi-
> cally correct 'outcomes'. (Campaign for Real Education, 2006)

Having set out a number of experiences and observations that demonstrate the highly contested and controversial nature of citizenship education itself, I will provide some definitional focus on what is meant by controversy, before seeking to respond to some of these concerns.

Defining controversy in the citizenship classroom

Before being in a position to tackle a controversial issue, the citizenship teacher ought to be able to understand what we mean by the term; indeed being offered the space and time to consider such issues reflectively would be an early cultural marker of a shift towards the authentic praxis advocated above. The Crick Report defined a controversial issue somewhat elusively as a topic 'about which there is no one fixed or universally held point of view' (QCA, 1998). This is perhaps helpful from the point of view of conceptual breadth and simplicity; however, it fails to capture the essence of what we grasp, almost intuitively, as a controversial issue. In other words, we tend to know one when we encounter it, or at least when we begin to discuss it with others.

Dearden (1981: p. 38) offers a more sophisticated formulation by suggesting that 'a matter is controversial if contrary views can be held on it without these views being contrary to reason'. This appeal to epistemic rationality is echoed in the notion of 'reasonable disagreement' (McLaughlin, 2003: p. 150). Such approaches, deriving as they do mainly from a positivistic paradigm, suggest that it ought to be quite easy to dispense in short order with a number of what might be termed the 'marquee controversies': were the Apollo moon landings a hoax? Does homeopathy have any effect beyond placebo? Does intelligent design offer an alternative explanation for speciation? Despite the fact that the scientific consensus and evidential base around these issues is clear, they remain 'controversial' in the popular discourse. Indeed, some readers may already be bridling if they themselves maintain positions around these issues that might be regarded as 'contrary to reason'. As Bailey (2010: p. 11) notes: 'Non-evidential—or perhaps non-critical—beliefs are impervious to contradictory findings and are, therefore, incapable of amendment by the introduction of evidence or criticism.'

There are further categories of controversy that are less open to resolution, more explicitly ethical or that cannot be resolved through reason or the scientific method alone (such as abortion, euthanasia and vivisection). Some excellent work around the exploration of ethical dilemmas is beginning to emerge in some schools in Scotland. Teachers are utilising Socratic dialogue, Philosophy for Children and introductory units in Epistemology, in order to provide a scaffold for the development of ideas, arguments and stances around the most ethically contested topics. Such learning and teaching is potentially complex in the classroom and demanding of teachers, often taking them into the sometimes pedagogically disconcerting realms of uncertainty and inexactness. However, for the same reasons they offer significant potential for the development of citizenship skills, values and dispositions.

Developing capacity for the teaching of controversial issues
Citizenship education as 'praxis'

The preceding observations serve to highlight a core concern in this chapter, namely that the very notion of '*practice*' seems somehow inadequate in relation to the teaching of controversial issues, given such a complex political, professional, pedagogical and philosophical backdrop. Merely setting out to train teachers in a *set of practices* appears to be woefully insufficient, particularly in relation to the ambitious goals of enhanced participation, power and agency that citizenship education claims to address. Effective training of the 'citizenship teacher' therefore implies formation in something more substantial than the kind of pedagogical skill-set that might normally be expressed in technically descriptive standards statements. For example, the Scottish Standard for Full Registration states that: 'Registered teachers have sufficient knowledge and understanding to fulfil their responsibilities for cross-curricular themes including citizenship ...' (GTCS, 2006a: p. 6). They should also 'know in detail about the principles of education for citizenship and encourage pupils to be active, critical and responsible citizens within a local, national, international and global context' (GTCS, 2006a: p. 19).

While helpful, such statements fail to convey the complex matrix of skills, knowledge and values implied in such educational processes. It might be more helpful to promote the notion of a formation based on *praxis*, understood as a deeper, more cyclical process that represents a reflexive relationship between ideas and actions. As one educationalist has recently noted, 'the emphasis on the *ends* of citizenship education has not been accompanied by an equally vigorous and informed debate over the *means*' (McCowan, 2009: p. 4). Addressing this lacuna has implications for the training and development of teachers with a particular responsibility for citizenship education, as well as the professional standards highlighted above.

In England this applies mainly to those specialist teachers engaged with citizenship as a discrete subject. However in Scotland, the clear intention of the citizenship framework (considered in more detail below) is that every teacher has responsibility. It seems to follow logically from this that all teachers in Scotland ought to feel prepared to a sufficient degree that they can address controversial issues both within the knowledge and understanding components of the citizenship framework, as well as controversial elements of their own areas of the curriculum. The relevant citizenship documentation for Scotland is relatively understated with regard to the training and development needs of the teaching workforce: opportunities for initial and in-service education are described *as* 'likely to be of value', *for* example, on matters such as:

- how to involve young people in decision making;
- supporting young people undertaking community placements;
- developing international links;
- *dealing with controversial issues in the classroom.* (LTS, 2002: p. 35, emphasis added)

The notably light touch and open-ended idiom of such recommendations can be situated in the context of the Scottish policy 'consensus' described previously. Recently this has been manifested in a series of policy documents that appear conspicuously to avoid an overly prescriptive approach; indeed, the definitive statement on citizenship education in Scotland remains the 2002 'Paper for *Discussion* and *Development*' (emphasis added). To those practitioners more used to centralised and detailed curriculum direction this may be refreshing. However, for all the merits of this approach to policy and curriculum development, grounded as it seems to be in positive assumptions about the professionalism of teachers, it can be vulnerable to other, more pressing policy priorities that may not be presented in the same spirit, such as centralised imperatives around improvements in literacy and numeracy, and the raising of attainment more generally. Moreover, it appears insufficient to simply recommend more Continuing Professional Development (CPD), without any corresponding elaboration of 'guidance for a theoretically argued position towards the kind of pedagogy envisaged' (Levinson, 2006: p. 1218). As a result, many schools and teachers may remain unclear about the finer aspects of practice that are required.

Is there a place for 'indoctrination'?

While the very mention of indoctrination might create alarm and defensiveness on the part of educators, especially when the accusers are parents, politicians or the media, there are those who are more sanguine about the concept and indeed who positively advocate its application in educational settings, or at the very least assert their right to refrain from providing balance at all times. Freire (1998: p. 93) states that he:

> cannot be a teacher if I do not perceive with ever greater clarity that my practice demands of me a definition about where I stand. A break with what is not right ethically. I must choose between one thing and another thing. I cannot be a teacher and be in favor of everyone and everything.

From Freire's viewpoint, taking a stance reflects a deeper pedagogical or ideological credo that outweighs the weaker imperative to offer 'balance' over particular issues.

Green (1972) adopts a related standpoint, suggesting explicitly that indoctrination 'Has a perfectly important role to play in education ... [and] may be useful as the prelude to teaching ... we need not offer reasons for every belief we think important for children and adults to hold' (Green, 1972: pp. 44–5; cited in Bailey, 2010). However, such views and practices are likely to provoke concern for many in education, fearing the kind of accusations described above. It is a very delicate line to tread, where on the one hand a certain amount of opinionated presentation and bias can act as pedagogical stimulus (as I believe I experienced from my teacher), and on the other there are all too many opportunities to either consciously or subconsciously influence pupils. There is also a sense that one's own biases and prejudices are more acceptable than another's. Even for very skilled teachers, conscientiously trying to avoid bias can be problematic. Cotton's study (2006) of how experienced geography teachers navigated controversial environmental issues found that:

> Their desire not to express their own views frequently led to the situation where these views were expressed indirectly in the form of questions, or by control of students' turns in discussion. Whilst these strategies enabled the teachers to avoid explicitly stating their views, such an indirect expression of attitudes may have been harder for the students to challenge than a direct argument presented by the teacher. (Cotton, 2006: p. 16)

Indoctrination can, of course, be exercised in less direct fashion. Stephen Law, in *The War for Children's Minds* (2006), suggests that a range of strategies are employed to manipulate young people towards conformity, including systems of punishment and reward, manipulative imagery (such as the polar bear photo described previously), control and censorship. The educational pursuit of such conformity may, of course, be conducted in the name of social cohesion or patriotism while being technically indistinguishable from less 'acceptable' forms of indoctrination.

This takes place in a wider educational culture that, driven by narrow or unimaginative systems of measurement and accountability, tends to be risk-averse; in such a context, teachers may be dissuaded (or may abdicate themselves) from addressing controversial issues. However, again there are potential checks and balances, so long as teachers are sufficiently prepared to recognise when they are required. More positively, teachers might opt in to such approaches if they can be persuaded of the benefits of controversy in pedagogy.

The citizenship framework in Scotland

While the Scottish citizenship education documentation does not say a great deal about the idea of controversial issues, what is there is laid out very clearly, including a rationale for the study of difficult issues which states: 'The complexity of modern society and the magnitude of the changes taking place within it sometimes threaten to overwhelm individuals' (LTS, 2002: p. 6).

There is also a concise yet illustrative section on the importance of skills development in relation to controversies, including: 'negotiation, compromise, awareness of the impact of conflict on the overall wellbeing of the community and the environment, and development of well-informed respect for differences between people' (LTS, 2002: p. 9).

This suggests a pedagogical emphasis on process, rather than a prescriptive approach that encourages teachers to tackle named controversial topics. This pedagogical distinction was noted by Stradling (1984: p. 123) who observed that:

> Some teachers include these issues in their teaching because they are topical and may be directly relevant to pupils' lives or

because they are major social, political or moral problems of our times which pupils ought to know something about … the issues are taught as ends in themselves. Other teachers adopt a more process orientated approach, focussing upon issues as a means to some other end. The issue is regarded as less important than the manner in which it is examined.

The major new curriculum framework (*A Curriculum for Excellence*) in Scotland is based, among other things, upon principles of flexibility and choice, and would seem to be open to Stradling's two approaches. For example, in the new science curriculum there is scope to address longstanding issues of concern such as genetic modification, or for reactive and opportunistic teaching and learning around topical science. I recently observed a Primary 6 (age group approximately 10 years old) science lesson in which a student led the pupils through an experiment on oil dispersal in water, based on the major pollution incident in the Gulf of Mexico in 2010. The science component was clearly linked to issues around environmental, economic and social impacts, and was designed to lead on to further discussion around the ethics and sustainability of deep sea drilling.

The fact that such practices are beginning to appear in the classroom is to my mind a very encouraging sign. A similar movement in the English context has recently been identified and praised:

> The better citizenship teachers ensured that students gained the knowledge they needed in order to have something worthwhile to say. They drew on topical issues, if necessary changing their detailed planning to accommodate these. They established clear ground rules for discussing controversial issues and were not frightened to do so. (OFSTED, 2010: p. 15)

However, it is arguably the case that the Scottish aspiration for a common agenda of good practice and shared responsibility across all teachers and sectors is not being fully realised, particularly when one compares the experience of pupils in primary and secondary settings. It seems, for example, that some of the positive momentum around citizenship more generally during the primary years appears to be lost in the transition to secondary schools (Deuchar, 2009).

Stradling (1984: pp. 124–5) listed a number of possible constraints on the teaching of controversial issues including those relating to the teacher, to the school, as well as those that were externally imposed and some that were issue-specific. It may be that some of these inhibitors are more influential in the secondary sector. The inevitable focus on examinations and attainment constitutes a significant barrier that is related to the teacher, the school and external pressures all together. This can be contrasted with the perceived greater freedom of discussion within the primary sector: 'Whereas some secondary teachers are often uncertain about whether some topics are suitable for younger children, most primary teachers feel that any topic can be explored as long as it is handled in the right way' (Deuchar, 2009: p. 29).

Yet the underlying philosophy, as well as some of the emerging detail, of *A Curriculum for Excellence* offers, at least in principle, the chance to extend such flexibility to the secondary sector, although the lack of confidence to do so is palpable among sections of the secondary community. In this, as in other respects, there is surely a role for a more coherent approach to these issues in teacher education across the full continuum from Initial Teacher Education to lifelong learning and CPD.

Conclusion

Given all the foregoing observations around the contested and controversial nature of citizenship education itself, and of the challenges of neutrality, it might be that the effective teaching of controversial issues is the preserve of the 'teaching wizard' (Hess, 2002: p. 38), the idealised teacher with almost superhuman and alchemic attributes. Alternatively, and more optimistically, it may be that these skills are achievable by any member of the teaching workforce, so long as the relevant training and development needs are identified and facilitated. However we still appear to be some way off a professional conception of the teacher that encapsulates these requirements. Even where such matters are highlighted, there is a worrying gap between aspiration are reality.

It is hard to see where, in the present arrangements for initial teacher education and induction there is sufficient time and space for beginning teachers to acquire this detailed knowledge. Furthermore, once they embark fully on their careers they operate in a wider educational context that confronts them with educational priorities and values that sometimes appear to be in conflict with the goals above. Changing models of teacher education, including a growing trend towards 'apprenticeship' models, might well bring some benefits through enhanced exposure to practice, but at the same time they tend to reduce the opportunity for the deeper intellectual engagement that I have advocated here as a prerequisite for authentic and effective teaching of controversial issues.

Why does all of this matter? Authentic democratic renewal requires a profound shift from traditional adversarial and remote forms of quasi-representative governance to more deliberative and inclusive democratic practices and structures, which in turn implies a need for a populace skilled and experienced in such deliberation and participation. The populace also has to be skilled in decoding information and applying evidence effectively in order to challenge power and orthodoxy. As Carl Sagan put it, 'Part of the duty of citizenship is not to be intimidated into conformity' (Sagan, 1996, p. 427). There is an unresolved tension between the minimalist vision of citizenship education that promotes conformity and passive responsibility, and a more challenging education for citizenship that fosters criticality, action and deliberation that might lead in some instances to non-conformity and the willingness to challenge.

The latter form of education for citizenship requires a kind of engagement with controversial issues as being more than simply 'topics for debate'. To be effective it needs the citizenship teacher and pupils alike to fully appreciate the grounds on which they can challenge particular points of view. It can only proceed fully through a blend of political, scientific, ethical and epistemological literacy.

Such a combination of literacies would, in the pithy words of Postman and Weingartner (quoted in Leighton, 2006), help us to foster 'experts in crap detecting'. In a world of increasing complexity, where information and opinion flows so prodigiously in so many unmediated forms, the need for such expertise is greater than ever.

Note

1 This was an extended industrial dispute across the UK and represented a significant milestone as a clash between neoliberal political and economic forces on the one hand and organised labour and the traditional left on the other.

Between Spaces of 'Otherness' and Belonging: Lessons on Global Citizenship and Controversy in the Classroom

Rita Verma

I want to express my religious identity and wear a turban in a public school—yet I am harassed, called a terrorist and told to go back to my country. (Sikh immigrant high school student in Queens, New York)

Jeffrey Conroy, 19, was one of seven teenagers from Patchogue, New York implicated in the November 2008 stabbing death of Marcelo Lucero in what prosecutors say was the culmination of an ongoing campaign of violence targeting Hispanics. The teens alluded to 'beaner-hopping' or 'Mexican hopping'. (CBS News 19 April 2010)

What is universal about Sikh immigrants being labeled 'terrorists', Muslim women feeling marginalised and exploited and hate crimes committed against Hispanic communities? These examples are testament to the tensions that arise between theoretical notions of citizenship under the global conditions of mobility and transnationality. Notions of citizenship and belonging are highly contested terrains since citizenship invariably implies assimilation. Citizenship is a lived experience and can foster contradictory and conflictual definitions of 'belonging' that can lead to exploitation, marginalisation and violence. Citizenship education often lacks the conversation on the origins of the definitions of 'Otherness' or how subject bodies become 'Other'. Global migration has increased diversity in most nation-states and is forcing nations to rethink citizenship and citizenship education. National boundaries are eroding because millions of people live in several nations and have multiple citizenships (Castles and Davidson, 2000). Millions have citizenship in one nation and live in another. Others are stateless, including millions of refugees around the world. The number of individuals living outside their original homelands increased from approximately 33 million in 1910 to 175 million in 2000 (Benhabib, 2004). In the American context, we continue to engage in an ideological, political and physical war on terror and have heated battles about the threat of immigrants among us who are seen as terrorist, illegal and/or the enemy of the state. Few opportunities are provided in school to 'unlearn' these ideological forms. Discourses about the 'Other' and exclusionary practices are deemed controversial and are consistently silenced in the curriculum. History is also generally taught from an ethnocentric viewpoint. Marginalised youth come to learn that their histories do not matter. Yet, these spaces between 'Otherness' and belonging are where negotiations take place for immigrant youth in transnational diasporas—whether of Sikh, Muslim or Hispanic descent. Identity politics become contested as youth are submerged in the push and pull of a desire for 'acceptance' and face the backlash of racist nativist sentiment. How are these lessons and ideological messages about citizenship negotiated by youth who are on the margins of the conversations? How can educators engage students on 'controversial' topics such as immigration, hate crimes and racism that can further encourage lessons on global citizenship and foster social activism? The manner students come to learn about other individuals and experiences that are different from their own can serve as an initial step outside the local and into the global. Based on classroom practice and ethnographic narratives on the experiences of Sikh youth, who originate from Northern India, in particular, these important questions will be explored.

The lessons taught about citizenship

Students understand deeply the injuries of race, class and gender oppression as they navigate through the educational system. Immigrant youth face added hardship as they are either harassed or told they do not belong and are repeatedly placed in remedial courses by a system that creates ranks and hierarchies that closely reflect the status quo. Theories of citizenship have been advanced, in the tradition of Western political theory, by white, heterosexual males who identified a homogenous citizenship through a process of systematic exclusion rather than inclusion in the polity (Torres, 1998). Identities of citizenship are denoted by normalised white, English-speaking members of European descent. Often, White, middle-class preservice (future) social studies teachers reproduce notions of what it means to be a full citizen that are based on a white standard and are part of an unacknowledged 'property' (privilege) of whiteness. Normalisation of citizenship to a white mainstream standard becomes the basis for teachers' production of civic identities and practice as civic educators. (Banks, 2008). The growing disconnect, both racially and culturally, between teachers and students, requires a serious consideration of the nation's public school message about compliance with such citizenship normalisation. The denial of social resources to US-born children of undocumented individuals, the detainment of suspect individuals in Guantanamo Bay, the execution of raids in Muslim mosques, or South Asian and Muslim neighbourhoods, and the enactment of the US Patriot Act represent various citizenship policies that have been recently adopted and warrant serious deconstruction and understanding. As Sunaina Maira (2005) has argued, this array of proposed citizenship policies represents an autocratic system about how citizenship should be constituted. Simultaneously, it implicitly structures a sense of citizenship surveillance in schools, communities, institutions and civil society. As Ladson-Billings (2004) and others in education have argued, citizenship in the US has taken place within a context of struggles and negotiations originating in a history of conquest and colonisation. Citizenship conceptions, identity and practices are thus historically grounded. Through our lack of critical intervention, we in essence become advocates of the knowledge, culture and ideas about citizenship that are determined by the textbook, and we strip away opportunities to ask why and to probe further. What are the real lessons here? A message is perhaps sent that we give more weight to half truths, untruths and fabrication and turn away opportunities to unearth realities, multiple perspectives and to be anti-oppressive and to teach life lessons. Michael Apple (2004) challenges educators everywhere to persist in the difficult, often painful, work of critically and honestly exploring the ideological assumptions and understandings that shape their work, and to confront how they themselves are implicated in the reproduction and maintenance of the dominant structure and organisation of schooling.

Historically, education has been a principal site for the reproduction and elaboration of racial meaning, racial identities and citizenship formation. An examination of racial discourses within the overall trajectory of curriculum and educational theories and practices rapidly disabuses us of the notion that education is a 'neutral' or 'innocent' institution with respect to racial struggles (JanMohamed, 1987). For example, commonly held beliefs by teachers, administrators and researchers in the field assume certain adaptation patterns to schooling for 'Asian American' immigrant children. This notion of popular racism is eloquently described by Fazal Rizvi (1993): 'popular racism is hegemonic because it expresses itself as an authoritative discourse inviting the kind of rhetorical appeal that is by its very nature uncritical'. Hidden curriculum in schooling becomes a vehicle for social control, and there is a perceived need to instill a common American culture and ideals about citizenship in the face of massive waves of immigration (Apple and Beane, 2007). These messages directly impact students self-confidence and esteem. Issues of self-esteem and 'fitting in' are critical in the formation of cultural identity, citizenship and feelings of belonging for students. In the words of Sonia Nieto (2002: p. 11), 'curriculums in many United States schools today are perceived by students as being irrelevant to their lives and experiences. As a result, these students become disengaged from school.' Nieto suggests educators need to examine the 'hidden curriculum' reflected in bulletin boards, extracurricular activities, and other messages given to students about their abilities and talents, and notes that such practices as tracking can be problematic, and that teachers should consider what practices work well with the cultures of the students they teach. Nieto asserts the many ways that a monocultural education disempowers students.

Painting a more accurate picture of what is happening in the world and understanding the complexity of issues like terrorism, immigration and cultural difference are integral to achieving a broader definition of citizenship. The celebration of core knowledge, for example, also excludes the voices and experiences of the immigrant communities of South Asia and the Middle East. Cameron McCarthy, in *The Uses of Culture: Education and the Limits of Ethnic Affiliation*, states that the production and negative arrangements of the third world in textbooks draws on the media language, and the media language is powerful and saturates popular culture both in and outside of school (McCarthy, 1998). Readings and lessons on the Middle East and South Asia are often excluded or form a minimal part of the curriculum. Moreover, there is a significant failure to disrupt emerging stereotypes. Islamophobia, or this irrational fear of or prejudice towards Muslims, is rarely disrupted due to lack of interest on the part of educators. With the absence of an informative curriculum about the factual histories of peoples of the Middle East and South Asia, Sikh and South Asian students (especially those who wear turbans), as well as Arab-Americans, in many ways become forced to 'teach' fellow students about their ethnic backgrounds. Ladson-Billings (2004) argues that the dynamic of the modern (or postmodern) nation-state makes identities as either an individual or a member of a group untenable. Rather than seeing the choice as either/or, the citizen of the nation state operates in the realism of both/and. One is both an individual who is entitled to citizen rights that permit one legally to challenge infringement of those rights and one who is acting as a member of a group. People move back and forth across many identities, and the way society responds to these identities either binds people together or alienates them from the civic culture. Diana Hess (2009) would further argue that such discussions on controversy, as posed by Ladson Billings, are critical. Hess argues that discussions, and particularly those that deal with controversy, are essential to a democracy.

Confronting controversial issues and tackling discourses of prejudice, injustice and hate may be uncomfortable, yet they should be central to developing curriculum and learning experiences that are democratic and globally connected. Within the social studies classroom it is critical to discuss the idea of global citizenship and one's responsibility to other communities. The history classroom, however, is often ethnocentric, which is a form of ignorance whereby a person finds it difficult to learn from another culture, already knowing it to be inferior. According to James Loewen (2010: p. 13), 'history can make us less ethnocentric, but as usually taught in middle and high school, it has the opposite effect. That's because our textbooks are shot through with the ideology called "American exceptionalism"—American exceptionalism promotes ethnocentrism.' Studies reveal that focusing course content on controversial topics positively affects students' attitudes toward citizen duty, political participation and political efficacy as well as their political trust, social integration and political interest.

I am 'other'

What politics are in place that racialise Sikh communities (from Northern India) in the United States? How do local/global events impact how we have come to know Sikh histories and experiences? This topic is important in social studies research, particularly in relation to how we can teach the local/global Other. I argue that decolonising mainstream knowledge about local/global issues requires a careful understanding of current Islamophobic and xenophobic attitudes. Historically, Eurocentric knowledge has influenced how people have come to know people who are considered different and who are seen as 'uncivilised'. Helping students learn through a global perspective is critical to unlearning racist ideologies that divide people. Contemporary political rhetoric over national security, which is often situated within discourses of terror and terrorism, often blames the foreign brownskinned 'Other' as the one to be feared. The immigrant background of most of the suspects and perpetrators of worldwide violence has contributed to the rise of Islamophobia and racial tensions in Europe and the United States. That students who fit a certain profile feel excluded only further suggests a need to bring their voices and histories into the curriculum. It is imperative that social studies educators understand cultural dimensions of global history and contemporary immigrant experiences. Sikh students have been racialised in schools in the post-9/11 period—a topic that is connected to the mission of social studies in teaching global citizenship and diversity, and I argue that by being knowledgeable about cultural histories and experiences we can be critical of prejudicial acts that have incited hatred in our school hallways, particularly in the post-9/11 context. As we continue to discuss what counts as 'legitimate knowledge' to be learned in school curriculum and who counts as a citizen, there has been little discussion on the need to educate students about the experiences of marginalised groups such as Sikhs.

It is worth noting Kellner's argument in regard to representations of the West versus the non-West; Kellner states that:

> the arbitrary line of demarcation is stabilised by the constant production and reproduction of attributions, differences, desires, and capacities that separate the West from the

non-West. The West is rational, the third world is not. The West is democratic, the third world is not. The West is virtuous, moral and the side of the good and right; the third world is vicious, immoral and on the side of evil. Indeed the electronic media images generated around United States' ongoing conflict with Iraq exploits precisely these dichotomies in order to help the American viewer separate the cause of the US and the West from that of the bad guys of the Middle East—Saddam Hussein and the Iraqis. (McCarthy, 1998: p. 36)

Osama bin Laden was then added to the list of 'evil-doers' and the irrationality of the 'third world'. As Cameron McCarthy (1998) reminds us, the production and negative arrangements of the third world in textbooks draws on the media language and the media language is powerful and saturates popular culture both in and outside of school. Taken together, the media has succeeded in reviving Anti-Arabism and Islamophobia in hegemonic discourse and this has incited a rise in hate crimes and racist backlash.

Consider the response of many of the Sikh youth who spoke about the immediate and personal impact of 9/11 on their lives:

Life's been hard after 9/11. That day had a profound effect on me, not only I felt sad but I was worried about my future in America. I came here by thinking that America is land of opportunities but now it's just a big question mark. I wonder if I will be appreciated in this country. As an immigrant, people are always going to give me the look. (Aman)

No, I do not feel American. I still feel very Indian. I think that we put out the flags since we do not want to look too obvious. But that has not helped. Even if we show our support, we still are being harassed and being targeted. (Balvinder)

Some of the girls grabbed my hair and pulled some strands out. They thought I was a Muslim girl and they thought I was evil. They kept shouting you are evil you are evil to me. I just started to cry and felt like I had nowhere to go. (Parminder)

As foreigners and 'brown folks' took the spotlight as the 'dangerous Other' in the 9/11 aftermath, so did the nature of identity politics within Sikh communities. Important measures were taken in order to disrupt the mounting hostility and ignorance about the community. A need for being recognised as 'good people' and as supportive community members and a refusal of the newly ascribed characteristics of being 'dangerous' was called for. The larger community desired to be viewed as peaceful and accepted, and they pushed to educate the larger public on the realities and distinctions of Sikhism. Multiple strategies of recognition were adopted within Sikh communities globally:

> You cannot educate anyone since the racism is everywhere. In
> India they kill you, in America they kill you, in England they
> kill you, you cannot escape. Violence is all around us. (Jasbir)

Aman did not agree: 'you can't just accept that that is the way-we have to fight for our rights. We are going to disappear- there will be no Sikhs left in the world then.'

Daily harassments, hate crimes, racism at the work place, violence and a general sense of feeling unwelcome ensued. In 2003, reports of hate crimes and racism targeted at Sikh Americans continued. A Hollywood film used the Sikh subject as a targeted community and this further demonstrated the failure truly to address the issue. *DisFunktional Family* was a movie starring the comedian Eddie Griffin, in which Griffin pointed to a turbaned elderly Sikh man walking on the street and shouts, 'Bin Laden, I knew you was around here!' The Sikh community signed a petition and pleaded for Miramax films to remove the scene from the movie in order to prevent backlash hate crimes. Miramax was not responsive. Where did the Patriot Act provide protection here? The youth were angered at the film and the fact that it was not reconsidered. At school, following the days of the release of the movie, Sikh youth were taunted with the same line that was used in the movie.

September 11 and schools

An alarming number of the post-9/11 incidents against Asian Americans occurred in the workplace and in schools. 'In a number of cases, students were the targets of racial slurs by their classmates, some were even physically attacked while in school' (*India Abroad* newspaper, 22 March 2002).

Schools became the prime vehicle for educating youth about 9/11 and for reproducing patriotism and loyalty to America. The aftermath of September 11 was punctuated by a renewed sense and eagerness to assert national belonging, and perhaps to eliminate those that were 'unpatriotic'. School policies of 'zero tolerance for intolerance' and efforts to address safety concerns for Arab students and those assumed to be of Arabic descent were largely unsuccessful, as evidenced by unending acts of violence and harassment of students to the present day. Schools have not been immune to the rise in racist nativism and hostile attitudes that ensued from the aftermath of the terrorist attacks. Many years after the attacks, the Sikh-based movement to educate the public on Sikhism continues. There were more American flags and increased discussion about 9/11, yet a weak attempt to distinguish or educate children about who specifically was responsible for the tragic day.

Mainstream students were quick to name 'Arabs', 'Muslims' or people from certain nations as dangerous and suspect. According to the youth, school officials did little to take the time to deconstruct an obvious and growing racism. Sikh youth were targeted as well, and were treated in unwelcome ways. In the 9/11 aftermath, however, Sikh youth described schools as places of conflict, tension and violence. The girls described how they liked to show off their long unshorn hair and that girls used to compliment them. Attitudes changed, however. Sikh youth began to make drastic decisions to avoid unwanted attention and hostility. Some of the young men who had turbans have cut their hair and no longer wear their turbans in school. They described that a rise in anger, jokes and rudeness that had been directed towards them triggered these decisions. Attempts to educate others in school about Sikhism were also unsuccessful. The racial slurs, harassment and unwelcome attitudes had great impact on the youth. Feelings of fear, anger and disillusionment surfaced. A world that was becoming familiar to them suddenly placed them as unwanted strangers.

Initially, the Sikh youth desired to educate other students and their teachers on the distinction of Sikhism from other cultures and religions. These efforts, however, did not lessen the racism and were not very well received. Since the initial attempts to disseminate knowledge after the attacks, the students had been silent. Youth depicted their reaction as one of 'self-silencing' in order to not bring unwanted attention upon them. Because of the prejudice they had faced, the youth pointed out how their parents had begun to question the seemingly value-free conceptions such as citizenship, justice and democracy in the United States. Similarly, the question of what constituted home and a sense of not belonging in India or in the United States was an issue that the youth felt they were now able to understand from their parents' experiences. The Sikh students' experiences help us understand how diverse students encounter more explicit forms of racism because of national and international events. Rizvi (1993) pointed out that racism ought to be viewed as a dynamic ideological construct that is continuously changing, being challenged, interrupted and reconstructed, and that it often operates in contradictory ways. Indeed, racial forms of prejudice are complex, multi-faceted and historically specific. Social studies educators have rightly pointed out how diverse immigrant students' racial experiences and cultural identities (racial, ethnic, religious, etc.) are often marginalised in school. Bhabha (1994) introduced the idea of 'in-between-ness' to capture the essence of the immigrants' paradoxical existence. The immigrant is viewed as living on the borderline, thus negotiating national and international, local and global identities. Das Gupta (1997: p. 45) stated that the 'in-between space that the Asian Indian immigrant occupies represents a transnational hybridity where the world of linkages and connections comes alive and throws all those concerned into the paroxysms of confusion and conflict'. How can emerging stereotypes be disrupted when youth feel that they are part of the problem or when discussions about their histories are deemed controversial?

Teaching 9/11: stereotypes affect us personally

> I guess I always think of terrorist when I see a man in a turban—
> does that mean I am a racist? (eighth grade student, Social
> Studies class)

Art, visual imagery and political cartoons can send powerful messages. The lessons that can be learned from these messages can have far reaching pedagogical relevance as well. These lessons are taught throughout the year to facilitate a year-long commitment and dialogue and are taught in a public school in a small homogenous community in New York. Eighth grade students were given a political cartoon to analyse critically. The exercise was not related directly to the class content and was intended to provide a lesson on stereotypes. Students spoke honestly and expressed that they might have asked similar questions of students who wear turbans. Is it offensive? Are they being racist and oppressive? Do they fear certain groups of people? Perhaps they were never provided the opportunity to verbalise their thoughts and now were exploring their own assumptions. As the teacher and class treaded on deep waters and began to ask the obvious questions about how we group people, why we judge them and the feelings and emotions we attach to certain labels, controversies spark and the ugly head of prejudice and stereotyping faced the entire class-room. The question then followed with the following inquiries: Who is an American? Who are our neighbours?

To further the discussion, the teacher showed the same cartoon with a young man with a baseball cap. Students began to laugh and say, 'Doesn't anyone know that a baseball cap is just an ordinary hat?' The connections began to be made. Students were then asked to think about an incident where they were judged incorrectly, and were asked to draw themselves similarly to the cartoon with questions that they were asked that they felt were offensive. This experiential learning exercise required the students to think about how they felt uncomfortable and, further, how a young man in a turban, or a similar physical adornment for that matter, might feel. Students came to understand that the cartoon represents apathy and igno-rance—whereas learning about someone's culture or asking in a mean-ingful respectful manner can transform it to empathetic and thoughtful questioning.

The political cartoon instigated a conversation that was then taken to many different levels as the class conducted a lesson on turban savvy and Islamophobia. When students came to learn that 80% of Sikh youth are harassed on a daily basis, for example in Queens, New York, it struck an emotional chord. Although images of Osama bin Laden may not appear on American television sets every evening as they did several years ago, the image has become part of American 'commonsense' and popular culture. This image has become ingrained in the immediate memories of the general public and has become a racialised stigma that continues to be used to target communities with hatred and violence. The term 'Taliban' has now become a racial slur and is used commonly against minority groups. Students were also engaged in a discussion about racial epithets. The discussion of experiences with racism provided a bridge for understanding because students shared their personal stories. Students spoke about their experiences with racism and their memories of feeling left out. Students shared examples of what was happening in school between different racial groups. In the middle school, students grouped themselves according to their racial background. As the class empathised with one another, they became individuals and not the stereotypes. It was important for everyone to hear different viewpoints. This is an example of how teaching in a pro-justice manner should be grounded in the lives of students and be hopeful, joyful, kind and visionary. Discussions should be critical, multicultural and globally connected, anti-racist and pro-justice, participatory, experiential, activist, academically rigorous, and culturally and linguistically sensitive.

To conclude the lessons on cultural identities and stereotypes, the teacher frequently encourages her students to use the medium of art to express their own cultural identities. Visual representations of self can provide powerful lessons and open up a safe space for students to share how they define themselves and the personal struggles they may face. The process of developing the artistic work is coupled with reflective essays and larger group discussions that ultimately become affirming and celebratory interactions. Media analysis, reflective writing, simple debates, role play simulations and critical inquiry can also be used. Although this may seem to be a simple example of engaging students in a controversial issue related to 9/11, it illustrates well the life lessons that can be learned when educators make it relevant and important to explore controversy in students' lives and the curriculum.

Conclusion: human rights and global citizenship

The goal of citizenship education should be to help students develop an identity and attachment to the global community and a human connection to people around the world. By making the oppression of students within the classroom relevant, students can learn about empathy and social justice towards one another. Students should be empowered by the understanding that they can make a difference and ought to engage in activism and human rights projects. Students must also develop a deep understanding of the need to take action as citizens of the global community and to make decisions to help solve the world's complex problems. Both educator and learner need to contribute in ways that will enhance democracy and endorse equality and social justice in their cultural communities, nations and regions, and in the world. Global identities, attachments and commitments constitute cosmopolitanism (Nussbaum, 2002). Cosmopolitans view themselves as citizens of the world who will make decisions and take actions in the global interests that will benefit humankind. Nussbaum (2002: p. 4) states that their 'allegiance is to the worldwide community of human beings'. Citizenship education should help students to realise that 'no local loyalty can ever justify forgetting that each human being has responsibilities to every other' (Appiah, 2006: p. xvi). A differentiated conception of citizenship, rather than a universal one, is needed to help marginalised groups attain civic equality and recognition in multicultural democratic nations (Young, 1989). Many problems result from a universal notion of citizenship according to which 'citizenship status transcends particularity and difference' and 'laws and rules ... are blind to individual and group differences' (Young, 1989: p. 250). It is equally imperative to bridge the study of 'domestic multiculturalism' to the international arena and globalisation. Across the board, our curriculums are deeply, globally disconnected. Creating those global connections, establishing the study of peace and human rights, and teaching for social justice can reveal limitless opportunities for students.

Educators must teach students that they are part of a globalised world—a much larger system than what they may know locally. These goals of citizenship education are inconsistent with the citizen's role in a global world today because many people have multiple national commitments and live in multiple nation-states. However, the development of citizens with global and cosmopolitan identities and commitments is contested in nation-states throughout the world because nationalism remain strong. Nationalism and globalisation coexist in tension worldwide (Castles and Davidson, 2000; Benhabib, 2004). When responding to the problems wrought by international migration, schools in multicultural nation-states must deal with complex educational issues in ways consistent with their democratic ideologies and declarations. There is a broad divide between the democratic ideals in Western nations and the teacher practices and curriculum and daily experiences of students in schools. Ethnic minority students in the United States, Canada, the United Kingdom, Germany and France—as in other nations throughout the world—often experience discrimination because of their cultural, linguistic, religious and value differences. Often, both students and teachers identify these students as the 'Other'. This is well illustrated by the narratives shared on Sikh immigrant youth.

Children in schools need to learn to be 'critical readers', as we can observe from the exercise presented with the political cartoons. A transformative process can commence as students begin to understand their rights and become inspired to advocate for others. A school-wide commitment to humanise education would require educators to play a critical role in bringing the community and the world into the classroom and expecting students to engage with them in deeply critical and serious ways. Within a history of global inequalities leading to the displacement and exodus of people, many migrants and immigrants act as social and civic citizens insofar as they contribute to the sociocultural and economic fabric of the nation in which they reside. Institutions normalise the citizenship identity of some subjects while subjugating others, depriving them of social and human rights. We need to believe that students can make a difference, become global citizens, that they can be part of social movements, and that they are a powerful and influential segment of society. The spaces between Otherness and belonging can be embraced by educators and provide ample opportunity for learners to be guided and nurtured to not only define selves but to open up the discussion to the larger classroom to understand how they are implicated in the dialogue as well.

Part III

Accountability and Education for Citizenship

Introduction to Part III:
Accountability and Education for Citizenship

Accountability systems send signals about what is valued in schooling. They are second-order ways of assessing the standard to which first order tasks are carried out, as Baroness Onora O'Neill indicated in her keynote address to the Annual Conference of the British Educational Research Association in London in September 2011. That is to say that indicators of standards, such as pupil attainment scores, are a proxy for the quality of teaching and learning taking place in classrooms. An accountability system in which attainment trumps all other purposes of schooling sends very clear messages to pupils, parents and teachers about the relative lack of importance of other long-held purposes of schooling such as social citizenship, health and well-being and critical autonomy. Moreover, the dominance of pupil attainment as the key indicator of school standards can have unintended consequences such as teaching to the test, the focus of teacher attention on pupils on the pass grade boundary to the detriment of others and 'massaging' test scores to improve a school's performance profile. Thus the second-order nature of the indicator can damage the quality of the first-order task—in this case teaching and learning—that it was designed to measure.

The pernicious impact of attainment as *the* key performance indicator of school standards is addressed in each of the chapters in this section. Pring, a philosopher of education, highlights the diverse aims of education and the impossibility of reducing them to easily quantifiable outcomes. Highlighting that education for citizenship goes beyond knowledge and understanding towards a proclivity to action, he argues that a system which measures only learning outcomes distorts the essential nature of education for citizenship. Like the other contributors in this section, Pring emphasises that pupils learn about citizenship by being active citizens and actively participating in decision-making about aspects of school life. Thus developing a democratic and participatory ethos is a key part of education for citizenship. This is not easily reducible to a measure.

Greer, a former chief inspector of schools and now Director of Education in Fife, Scotland, echoes Pring in his emphasis on the importance of process, arguing that one cannot 'inspect citizenship in' as it is always possible to have superficial compliance with processes. It is the quality of the process which is important. Greer gives an account of the development of inspection and accountability of schooling, and notes the move from a 'top-down' compliance culture from national to local government and from local government to schools, to a culture which focuses more on collaborative working for improvement through robust school self-evaluation.

An experienced headteacher of primary schools, Peacock describes the development of Wroxham School from one which had lost all sense of agency and was downtrodden by its poor performance in terms of attainment outcomes, to one fully engaged with its community. The journey involved moving from a competitive learning environment to a collaborative and cooperative one. Listening to the views of pupils, taking these views seriously and empowering teachers were key and Peacock describes the ways in which a democratic and participatory ethos became embedded within the school. Citizenship became a way of being and attainment improved. Peacock is modest about her role as headteacher, actively engaged with research and eager to learn from and contribute to understanding of education for citizenship. She finds the new inspection framework in England to be outward looking and supportive, but worries about its longevity in a new political climate.

The key questions for this theme are:
- How can a system accountability be moulded to support hard-to-measure purposes of schooling such as education for citizenship?
- Is robust school self-evaluation the desirable way forward and, if so, how is this to be supported?
- Is it useful to distinguish short-term and long-term effectiveness of education for citizenship? Can schools realistically be held accountable for the democratic health of the countries in which they operate?

Accountability, Assessment and Education for Citizenship

Richard Pring

Introduction

There are two related problems which I want to address in this chapter.

The first concerns the relationship between democracy and citizenship. In so doing, I argue that a failure to explore this relationship has created an impoverished understanding of the teaching of citizenship. It has removed it from the broader vision of education which is embedded in the teaching of the humanities and the arts. On the other hand, one must be careful not to freeze any analysis in a single definition of either democracy or citizenship. The meaning of a word lies in its use within a language more broadly, and that language evolves in its reflection of a wider form of life. Words and their meaning have historical roots—roots, that is, in social, economic and political forms of life which are themselves constantly evolving. 'Democracy', as a concept, does not remain static.

The second concern lies in the distortion which such concepts suffer from where education itself is in the grip of a way of seeing things from a particular management point of view. Managing the system of education has rendered it accountable in a particular way. That in turn shapes the function, and in turn the meaning, of assessment. I raise the question, therefore, about how one might reconcile accountability, as it is currently conceived, with a defensible view about education for citizenship within a democratic society.

Educational aims, democracy and citizenship
Aims of education

There have been many initiatives from Government in England in order, first, to improve standards, and, second, to enable the educational service in schools and colleges of further education to contribute more effectively to an improved economy in a very competitive world.

Therefore, first of all, much importance was attached to the Leitch Review (2006), which was interpreted as saying that there would be a massive reduction in the jobs available for those who had no qualifications or very low-level qualifications. Hence, the education and training system needed to be sharpened up to make this economic transfer possible—a better-educated and better-trained work force reflected in the increased higher-level qualifications awarded.

Second, focus has been placed upon the improvement of grades in the public examinations—for example, five A–Cs in the General Certificate of Education, including maths and English—and that has been reinforced by public announcement of Ofsted judgements, published grades, league tables of schools and announcements of failing schools.

A wider view of educational goals is reflected in the introduction of citizenship as a required subject in secondary schools, but the significance of this is submerged beneath the aims of improved standards, as these are measured in public examinations, and of serving the general economic well-being. Indeed, citizenship holds its own rather tenuously by becoming another subject with measurable targets and by its contribution to the overall grade scores.

All this, reflected in so many Government papers and initiatives, has been pursued without a prolonged discussion about the aims of education and about the educational values which should be embodied in educational practice. Such values and aims, therefore, are often only implicit (and therefore unexamined) in the practices of schools and colleges, and in the legislation and regulations of central government. And yet values have been implicit in so many of the significant decisions made—for example, in the decision to make the arts and humanities voluntary after the age of 14, in the dominance of forms of assessment which downgrade the significance of practical learning, in the curtailment of fieldwork despite its crucial contribution to forms of understanding in, say, geography (and, one might add, in citizenship), in the coverage of syllabuses such that there is little room for open discussion and disagreement.

Therefore, since education is taken as self-evidently a public good to which all young people should have access, it is important to ask: 'what are the public goods—the qualities, understandings, knowledge, attitudes and virtues—which should be fostered by educational programmes?'. Or, in the words of the Nuffield Review of 14–19 Year Olds, *What counts as an educated 19 year old in this day and age?* The raising of standards in terms of increased grades and the contribution to a more skills and knowledge-based economy seem too narrow. Much more is required of an educated person (cf. Pring *et al.*, 2009: pp. 12ff.).

'Educated' is an evaluative term. It indicates that the 'educated person' has developed through the acquisition of certain qualities and understandings. He or she is thereby a better person. Therefore, deliberation about educational aims and values is essentially an ethical matter. How do we decide what is educationally valuable? What sorts of characteristics should we be looking for and, through the system of education or educational programmes, be trying to nurture? What is it that makes us distinctively human, how did we become so and how can we become more so?—the three questions which Jerome Bruner (1966) argued should structure the social studies within schools.

The following would seem to be the features of being, and of developing as, a person, although, as in all ethical matters, there would not be consensus over the detail. 'Education' is a contested concept.

First, to educate would be to initiate the learners into the *knowledge and understanding* which enables them to live more fully human lives (what John Dewey referred to as 'the intelligent management of life'). Such an intelligent management of life requires a grasp of those concepts, principles and modes of enquiry through which we have come to understand the physical, social and economic worlds which we have inherited. The philosopher Michael Oakeshott (1989) referred to the initiation into the 'conversation between the generations of mankind' in which the young persons come to appreciate the different voices of poetry, philosophy, history, sciences and so on. And such voices are accessible to all at some level of understanding.

Second, to educate would be to recognise the young learners as 'doers', not just thinkers, in need for those *practical capabilities* which enable them to flourish both as individuals and within the broader social and economic community. Intelligence lies in 'knowing how' as much as in 'knowing that'.

Third, what distinguishes us as persons is the capacity to think and choose responsibly about the life worth living, about relationships with other people and about the 'big issues' which confront society (for example, social justice, racism, environmental change). 'Education' is concerned not only about knowledge and understanding, theoretical or practical, but about the development of *moral seriousness*.

Fourth, development as a person requires the recognition of *belonging to a wider community*—an inherited culture from which one gains a particular identity, support and sustenance, and which, in return, one is able to support and sustain. Each is a social animal, not a totally autonomous person. For each of us to flourish there is a need for the wider society in which to flourish, in terms not simply of economic well-being but also and especially of shared values, culture and aspirations.

Although these four areas of educational aim have been introduced separately for purposes of analysis, there is interdependence in their development. The development as a social being requires practical capability and cannot be reduced to mere knowledge and understanding. Furthermore, its direction is determined by the degree of moral seriousness—the extent, for example, to which a sense of justice and fairness enter into one's social relationships and civil aspirations. Such a holistic understanding of what it means to be and to develop as a person affects profoundly the aims of education, and challenges the very partial and impoverished aims which, though rarely examined, underpin policies concerned with 'raising standards' and 'economic well-being'.

The following two sections seek to develop and illustrate this point.

Education, community and culture

In *Democracy and Education*, John Dewey refers to 'education' as a 'social function, securing direction and development in the immature through their participation in the life of the group to which they belong' (Dewey, 1916: p. 83).

As argued above, part of what it means to be a person, and thus to develop as such, is to be part of a wider community from which one has acquired a way of seeing the world, of valuing particular ways of living, of communicating. That community may be primarily the family or the village in which the family is situated. But it may well be a wider network of people which shares a particular form of life—a religious form of life, for example. What brings the different individuals and families together is some common culture—a common way of seeing the world and valuing certain aspects of it. There are shared meanings and valuings. As Dewey pointed out: 'Men live in a community in virtue of the things which they have in common. What they must have in common in order to form a community or society are aims, beliefs, aspirations, knowledge—a common understanding—likemindedness as the sociologists say' (Dewey, 1916: p. 4).

The wider society in which individuals and their families live might or might not be a community. That is, the transactions between members (buying and selling goods, for example) may require only the minimum of shared values. Such transactions are externally enforced through the laws which are backed up by a penal system. Indeed, between people in the wider society there may be little of shared values, understanding, aims or aspirations. Furthermore, as the Chief Rabbi, Jonathan Sacks argues, the wider society consists of many different communities, sometimes with little in common between them—indeed, hostilities and distrust between them: 'a confusing mixture of reasons and associations which emerge, like a great river from its countless streams and tributaries, out of a vast range of histories and traditions' (Sacks, 1997: p. 55).

One might see these 'countless streams and tributaries' either as an enrichment of the wider society or as a contribution to its fragmentation – to its not being a community at all, but rather a collection of 'self-seeking individuals' or groups of individuals, with few or no shared values and aspirations.

Therefore, the 'social function of education' is to nurture the enrichment afforded by these 'countless streams and tributaries'. It is to note and to enhance what, beneath the differences, people have in common and what therefore, when developed, might provide the better basis for social and individual well-being. R. H. Tawney, in his book, *Equality*, highly influential on Labour Party thinking, argued thus:

> in spite of their varying character and capacities, men possess
> in their common humanity a quality which is worth cultivating
> and ... a community is most likely to make the most of that

quality if it takes it into account in planning its economic organisation and social institutions—if it stresses lightly differences
of wealth and birth and social position, and establishes on firm
foundations institutions [schools] which meet common needs,
and are a source of common enlightenment and common
enjoyment. (Tawney, 1938: pp. 55–6)

Hence, the significance of Dewey's idea of education as a 'social function'. Through education, the learners come to see the wider social contexts
in which their lives have emerged and might flourish. They see their own
particular communities to be inseparable from the wider communities
which themselves emerge from 'a vast range of histories and traditions'.
They come to see the interconnectedness of the different social networks
which constitute the wider society, and, in a period of global communication and movement, what one might refer to as the 'world community'.
Therefore, the school was seen as an extension of the group to which the
learners belong, enabling the kind of growth that the family is too limited
to provide. The school should anticipate the wider community into which
the young people were growing, and enable them to contribute to, to
enrich and to shape that community. As Dewey argued:

Roughly speaking, [schools] come into existence when social
traditions are so complex that a considerable part of the social
store is committed to writing and transmitted through written
symbols … As soon as a community depends to any considerable extent upon what lies beyond its own territory and its
own immediate generation, it must rely upon the set agency of
schools to insure adequate transmission of all its resources …
Hence, a special mode of intercourse is instituted, the school,
to care for such matters. (Dewey, 1916: p. 19)

Thus, the school was where people learn to appreciate and to understand
the different ways of seeing the world, to enter into the conversations
through which they deepen that understanding and to become enriched
by what others have said and done. If people or communities of people
within the wider society are to cooperate together and to live in harmony,

then there would be a need for society to educate its members to see what is common between them and to foster a sense of community that bridged the different ones to which they belong.

However, the communication and responsiveness associated with community do not and should not entail consensus. The benefits and strengths of community lie in the communication of differences, and thereby in the growth of that community through the seriousness with which those differences are addressed, reflected upon and modified. But even that serious sharing and addressing of differences requires a sense of community at a different level—an understanding that, beyond the differences, there lie commonalities of value and aim, which bring them together—a common culture, if you like, paradoxically both transcending and compatible with the coexistence of diverse cultures, arrived at through the meaningful interactions of the members.

Descriptively, culture embraces those shared practices, and the understandings and values embedded within those practices, through which groups of people make sense of experience, value certain things and activities, are able to anticipate how others see things and attribute particular significance or meaning to them. Culture, in its evaluative sense, refers to those values and understandings, embedded in certain practices, which are seen to enhance the distinctively human capacity for understanding, feeling, relating, adapting and contributing to the wider community.

This, however, is not easy and is indeed neglected in the pursuit of educational aims as they are explicitly or implicitly embedded in education policy and practice. As Halsey, who had been a powerful influence in the development of the comprehensive system of education, argued in his Reith Lectures: 'We have still to provide a common experience of citizenship in childhood and old age, in work and play, and in health and sickness. We have still in short, to develop a common culture to replace the divided culture of class and status' (Halsey, 1978).

One central feature, therefore, of education for citizenship is the development of a common culture—those understandings and values, which, though compatible with differences arising from communities with different beliefs and traditions, enable people to live and work together, to learn from each other, to overcome differences with a view to common aims arising from the recognition of a common humanity.

Education, democracy and citizenship

One main aim of education, therefore, is to create within the school community the opportunities for all young people to participate in that culture which enables them to make sense of the physical, social, economic and moral worlds they inhabit. That requires not only access to those different forms of knowledge, understanding and practice, but also the openness to others' interpretations and experiences. Other learners come from different backgrounds and other traditions. Their voices are of equal importance in our attempts to understand the world in which we live.

The ability, the disposition and the opportunity to communicate those experiences and to listen to others' accounts and corrections is the foundation of, and necessary ingredient in, a democratic community. Genuine communication requires reciprocity and mutual respect. Each person is of equal value, whose views and experiences need to be taken seriously, even if, through critical discussion, they are shown to be mistaken. Democracy entails freedom of action, but that freedom of action requires freedom of thought and the disposition to be open to the often different viewpoints of others within the community. Education should not only provide the intellectual and cultural resources with which to make sense of those experiences, but also space within which that 'making sense' can be achieved, namely, the community of learners who are actively engaged in discussion, enquiry, problem solving and practical pursuits.

That, then, is the aspect of democracy which is at the centre of education, namely, the community where there is maximum participation possible in deliberations about all matters affecting the lives of the learners and in the decisions arising from those deliberations. Nothing less shows the respect for the dignity of everybody. And schools should be the places where, through such a democratic community, young people acquire the knowledge, openness of mind and dispositions required for participation in and strengthening of the democratic community they will be entering as adults.

Such deliberations are enriched by the very diversity of experience and beliefs to be found within the classroom. We all grow through the challenges we receive to the ideas through which we view the world, if we have developed the intellectual virtues of openness of mind and if the atmosphere has been created in the school or university for deliberation about, rather than for defending, one's cherished ideas. Our ideas need constantly to be adapted to new ideas, new experiences and critical challenge. But that requires the creation of the context in which that can take place.

The democratic classroom was, therefore, central to Dewey's notion of education for citizenship. For Dewey, a citizen is the member of a community in which the interest of each and every one counts equally, in which each has a voice in saying what those interests are, and in which each has a place in the deliberations and decisions based on reconciling the interests of everyone. Dewey would have welcomed the creation of ESSA, the international student pressure group which is seeking student representation on the governing bodies of schools and active student councils. Democracy, so understood, is wider than any political arrangement. It is a moral ideal, based upon respect for each individual, upon the active participation of the individual in matters which concern them and the community to which they belong, and upon the formation of each individual for these purposes through education. Political arrangements are there to serve such practices; they are not the end or meaning of democracy.

Citizenship education in practice
The Crick Report (QCA, 1998) in England was in many ways an important landmark. It recommended 'citizenship' as an obligatory element within the curriculum for all young people. In so doing, it followed the arguments put forward by Bernard Crick over many years for political education in schools. If crucial to the well-being of each is that our communities, central and local, should be democratic, then it is crucial to have the future generation educated in democratic principles and be so motivated as to put them into practice. Central to such education should be an understanding of such basic concepts as 'political authority', 'democracy' and 'justice', as well as the ability to apply such concepts in the appropriate contexts. Crick referred to the acquisition of such concepts as 'political literacy' (cf. Crick and Porter, 1978).

Some would see the development of political literacy so conceived as the essence of political education for citizenship. But, according to Porter, a research colleague of Crick's: 'Political literacy would be limited to a solitary intellectual exercise; the politically literate person would merely be capable of well-informed observation and analysis. The ultimate test of political education lies in creating a proclivity to action' (Porter, 1979: p. 39).

Hence, political education should include 'political literacy', 'the proclivity to action' and, more, 'the procedural values', namely, those values or virtues which pertain to the kind of political argument which is concerned with getting at the truth—respect for reason, tolerance of dissent, concern for fairness in allowing everyone, especially the most vulnerable, to contribute.

Here certainly would seem to be the germs of the democratic learning community which Dewey saw to be the central aim of education. And yet there are problems, both theoretical and practical.

First, with regard to the proclivity to action, on the correct assumption that, just as being democratic and a citizen is a practical activity requiring practical know-how and intelligence, so the engagement in the practice of democracy would seem to be crucial. One learns how to do things by doing. An excellent example of this would be the creation of Kohlberg's 'just community school'. Lawrence Kohlberg at the Center for Moral Development at Harvard University had mapped out the stages of moral development, based on the central understanding of justice and fairness in the deliberations about what one ought to do. By trying to solve certain moral dilemmas, so the learners would develop their capacity to think according to principles, ultimately those principles which one would be prepared to make universal principles of practice. One major problem, however, was that young people could score high on the moral thinking tests without necessarily following through that thinking in practice. What was necessary was that those principles should be embedded in the institutional context of the learners. There is little point in teaching the principles and understanding of justice, if the daily experience of the young people was that of injustice. Dewey and his colleagues therefore established what was called the 'just community school' in which the students themselves play an active part in the decisions and deliberations which affected them. As Kohlberg said: 'In summary, the current demand for moral education is a demand that our society becomes more of a just community. If our society is to become a more just community, it needs

democratic schools. This was the demand and dream of John Dewey'
(Kohlberg, 1982: p. 24).

However, it is not easy to see many of our schools emulating Kohlberg's
Just Community School.

Perhaps that practical engagement in democratically conceived activities might be possible. But there are inevitable dangers and difficulties.
Eric Midwinter, working in inner city Liverpool in the 1970s, questioned
the prevailing benchmark of a successful school as that which enabled
young people to *escape* from their deprived communities. He pointed to
the oddness of educational success lying in the escape of a small minority
from their very family and community background. Rather should success
be measured in terms of how that education provided the consciousness
whereby that community might be transformed into something better. He
argued: 'As a theoretical goal we had defined the community school as one
which ventured out into and welcomed the community until a visionary
time arrived when it was difficult to distinguish school from community'
(Midwinter, 1975: p. 160).

This, however, creates a dilemma. The common school is the neighbourhood school, and as such it reflects a particular kind of community,
unlike and cut off from other communities that, in simple social and
economic opportunity terms, might be much more liberating. It might be
common solely to those within the deprived neighbourhood, reflecting the
depressed hopes and lack of aspiration of that community. But Midwinter's
solution would have gladdened the heart of John Dewey, namely, to centre
the organisation of learning around the intelligent response to that deprivation—helping them 'to manage their lives more intelligently'. For
Midwinter, education, far from being a means of escape, provided the
skills, understandings and dispositions to transform those very communities. He got the students to engage in community projects and be political
activists (researching social problems, identifying the means to overcome
them, campaigning for public support and taking action). Inevitably, this
excellent bit of citizenship education, because challenging the political
powers, was closed down.

A further example to illustrate both what might be meant by citizenship education and what are the difficulties in putting it into practice where
it is linked to the 'propensity to action', is that provided by Chris Searle.

Searle taught disadvantaged students (many of them black) in a Hackney comprehensive school how to express their feelings through their own creative writing and to explore the conditions under which they lived. The teachers started a printing press and a bookshop, and, together with the students, produced a journal *Teaching London Kids* as well as a book of poetry, *Stepney Words*. The journal became the voice of disillusioned young people, profoundly political in its content and tone. It was a vehicle by which these young people might find a voice amongst those who decide their future. But Searle was sacked from his school for publishing the students' voices in *Teaching London Kids* (cf. Searle, 1975).

In ensuring that 'citizenship' would be part of the curriculum (thus meeting the broader aims of education referred to above) it has been introduced as a subject (to give it extra force in a system which requires schools to be accountable in terms of the number of subject grades acquired).

Assessment and accountability

Educational aims permeate policy and practice, shaping what is to be done and determining what is acceptable. But, as argued at the beginning, such aims are rarely made explicit and thus rarely subjected to critical scrutiny. The broader educational aims, arising from what it means to be and to develop as a person and calling for a wider vision of learning, emphasise not only the development of knowledge and understanding (for example, political literacy) but also practical capability, moral seriousness and commitment to civil or community involvement.

However, aims, though not explicit, are embedded in the very language used. Our thinking is shaped by language; the concepts through which we understand the world are learnt through the use of words. Public services of all sorts have been transformed in recent decades by a managerial and business-related language which in turn transforms our understanding of them. In particular, there has been a shift in the language of education which affects how we understand what it means to learn and to teach, what is the relationship between teacher and learner, and what counts as a successful school.

Different metaphors come to dominate the discourse. The language of performance management finds little place for Oakeshott's 'conversation between the generations of mankind', in which the young learners come to appreciate and enjoy the voices of poetry, drama, science and philosophy. The language of *targets* and *measurable outcomes* seems incompatible with the kind of open-ended discussion in which the experiences and the voices of the learners, coming from different backgrounds and traditions, can have a respected place.

The teachers, pressured to meet the targets set by others who know not the learners, become the *deliverers of the curriculum*, not the mediators of an inherited culture, providing insights to learners with their own dominant and distinctive interests, concerns and understandings. These learners become the *customers* or *clients* in a service which is dominated by *performance indicators* and *audits* of that performance.

This language is the language of accountability, ensuring that schools and colleges, serving quite diverse communities with very different backgrounds and experiences, perform in a particular way. The right kind of outcomes is predetermined. Specific ground has to be covered in the curriculum. Many young people are thereby destined to fail, howsoever hard they have tried to understand or whatever contribution they have made to the deliberations on significant personal and civic issues. There is little room in such accountability for the 'proclivity to action'—for the active engagement in political activity or social change within their communities. Systematic discussion of matters of personal and social significance, with all the learning thereby taking place, becomes a luxury rather than a central curriculum activity.

If the broader aims of education to do with growth and development as a person are to be taken seriously, then the dominance of a particular form of assessment and accountability needs to be changed. There are limits to how far one ought to assess that learning which is most significant for young people—the slow struggle to understand complex issues, the personal transformation arising from the appreciation of a poem, the growing self-confidence emerging from a public performance, the thoughtful contribution to group deliberations over a controversial issue, the intelligent reflection upon significant experiences.

Such change is possible, but it needs a shift from target-based assessment to one in which evidence of significant learning is provided by the learner and in which there is greater scope for teacher assessment in the light of evidence with a view to helping the learner. There is a need to separate such assessment for learning from assessment for accountability. Only then will there be the kind of education for citizenship within the necessary democratic conditions outlined in this chapter.

Getting the Society we Deserve:
Accountability for Citizenship Education

Ken Greer

By maintaining a sound system of education you produce citizens of good character, and citizens of sound character, with the advantage of a good education, produce in turn children better than themselves. (Plato)

The twenty-first century: a new age for accountability and education for citizenship in Scotland

In Scotland, the first decade of the twenty-first century saw the codification of national structures to ensure continuous improvement in the delivery of public services. A rational system of accountability was developed which strengthened the capacity of government, both local and national, to take steps to ensure improvement where it was required. This accountability framework was particularly focused on education, which was seen to be a key to the achievement of a number of Scottish Government priorities. In parallel, there has been an upsurge of interest in education for citizenship in Scotland. The Scottish approach is to deliver citizenship education, not through timetabled inclusion of particular curricular inputs on civics, but through the embedded experiences learners have in schools and their opportunities to reflect on roles, rights and responsibilities.

The 1998 Scotland Act and subsequent establishment of the Scottish Parliament reflected and amplified interest in issues of nationality, governance and citizenship. The opportunity for a re-evaluation of national policies and traditions was embraced by the Scottish Parliament. In matters of school education policy there was a drive to establish a rational approach with clearly defined roles and responsibilities. The Act reflected a belief that the key to improvement was a clear chain of accountability stretching from the Minister's to learners' desks. In June 2000 the Scottish Parliament passed the Standards in Scotland's Schools etc. Act, testament to a belief in the potential of education to drive personal, social and economic improvement.

This accountability process positioned responsibility for raising standards in line with nationally agreed priorities and 'securing [school] improvement' with the education authority, as the provider of education through its schools. Each of Scotland's 32 authorities would set council-wide improvement objectives which would be supported by a development plan for each school. The education authority had the duty to 'define and publish measures and standards of performance' for the schools it managed and to act to bring about improvement. Schools and managing education authorities were subject to external inspection by Scotland's inspection agency, Her Majesty's Inspectorate of Education (HMIE). The Act prescribed a neat chain of accountability of teacher to school, school to managing authority and managing authority, through the work of government inspectors, to national government and through them to the citizenry as users and funders of schools.

In relation to its work in developing countries, the World Bank describes this approach as 'long route' accountability. In Scotland, HMIE, as the watchdog of national government, inspects and comments upon provision made by individual establishments and managing education authorities. Their findings are summarised in 'state of the nation' reports published on a 3–4 year cycle. Within the chain of accountability Scotland's education authorities have responsibility for ensuring the quality of provision in the schools they manage. Education authorities fulfil this role through continuous engagement, focused on challenge and support to the schools they manage, including formal evaluation activity. Each school is expected to self-evaluate as a basis for planning improvement, reporting annually on the standards and quality achieved.

The impact of HMIE's work results not from its processes, but from the uses to which inspection judgements are put. Education providers tend to be very responsive to HMIE reports. The policy of HMIE 'following through' inspection reports where provision has been evaluated to be in need of improvement suggests an assumption that without external intervention required improvements might not follow.

From the point of view of the practitioner, or those within the accountability chain, this 'rational' approach can appear to be less about due accountability and more about (tiresome) accounting. The changes in roles and responsibilities in the decade following the 2000 Act mean that *accountability* might be better expressed now as a *web* rather than *chain* of responsibility. The accountability landscape in Scotland is complex and fluid, a consequence of:

- blurring and re-aligning of roles and responsibilities (local authorities, Education Scotland, Scottish Government);
- changes in curriculum, inspection and review approaches;
- changing perceptions about accountability across government and the public sector;
- the use of practitioners to perform inspection roles (for example, the use by HMIE of 'associate assessors');
- multi-agency and partnership approaches to public service delivery;
- evolving models of governance, particularly in services for children;
- economic necessity.

Accountability intensifies as the focus for scrutiny is tightened. Understandably, parents are more interested in the outcomes for their own child's class than they are about those for a randomly-sampled cohort. As the new accountability model has developed in Scotland, it has been clear that the system needed to be capable of evolving rapidly in response to changing political and social imperatives. Onora O'Neill explored the prevailing culture of long-route accountability in public life in the UK in her 2002 Reith Lectures *A Question of Trust*. She called for 'more attention to good governance and fewer fantasies about total control' (O'Neill, 2002). In the third of her lectures, 'Called to Account', she questioned the audit and accountability culture:

> The new accountability has quite sharp teeth. Performance is monitored and subjected to quality control and quality assurance. The idea of audit has been exported from its original financial context to cover ever more detailed scrutiny of non-financial processes and systems. Performance indicators are

used to measure adequate and inadequate performance with *supposed* precision. This *audit explosion*, as Michael Power has so aptly called it, has often displaced or marginalised older systems of accountability.

The Scottish educational accountability framework was explored by Cowie and Croxford (2007). Reflecting on the Scottish Government's 'systems of tough, intelligent accountability', they questioned the primacy accorded to measuring attainment in the context of the principles under-pinning *Curriculum for Excellence*, such as greater freedom and creativity for practitioners, more curriculum personalisation for learners. Their conclusion that 'policy makers and HMIE will need to share control of the accountability system' describes a process which foreshadows the establishment in July 2011 of Education Scotland, the national education agency. It also resonates with the Crerar review (Crerar, 2007) into issues of public scrutiny and complaints handling.

For outside agencies to work effectively with schools, there needs to be consensus about educational priorities. In December 2000 the Scottish Executive produced the first (and to date only) set of National Priorities, intended to give 'strategic direction to school education' (HMIE, 2006c). Two of these priorities were:

> *Values and citizenship*: To work with parents to teach pupils respect for self and one another and their interdependence with other members of their neighbourhood and teach them the duties and responsibilities of citizenship in a democratic society.
>
> *Learning for life*: To equip pupils with the foundation skills, attitudes and expectations necessary to prosper in a changing society and to encourage creativity and ambition.

The national priorities illustrated the then Scottish Executive's com-mitment to education for citizenship. They were also associated with an undertaking to measure and report progress. In relation to education for citizenship, the strong support for the broad agenda represented by the National Priorities was not matched by a consensus about what would need to change in schools' practice. In their 2006 report on progress HMIE noted that:

> While national priorities set a broad vision for Scottish education, they have been less successful in setting meaningful outcome measures . . . Furthermore, the impact of some national priorities can only be measured in the long term with regard to improved levels of health, continued engagement in lifelong learning and more active participation in the democratic process by the adult population. (HMIE, 2006c: p. 4)

The timescale for measuring the impacts of citizenship education was seen as generational rather than annual. Accountability measures relating to citizenship education therefore tend to focus on potentially arbitrary judgements about school ethos, and learners' experiences. Reliable judgements are dependent on better longitudinal evaluation.

In March 2002, the Scottish Executive launched a national debate about the nature and purposes of education. Their response was announced in January 2003 (SEED, 2003), to include a review of the school curriculum which led to the development of *(A) Curriculum for Excellence,* which was seen to be the vehicle for supporting the achievement of the national priorities, redefined and expressed as four 'outcomes' or 'capacities' for children and young people: successful learners, confident individuals, responsible citizens and effective contributors. Education for citizenship was embedded within the aspirations of the new organic curriculum, to be developed collaboratively by teachers in schools guided by high-level guidance with minimal prescription of inputs, but with a clear focus on the active engagement of learners and their experiences. This approach involved entrusting and empowering teachers and schools in order to improve learners' experiences, attainments and achievements.

Ambitious, Excellent Schools (Scottish Executive, 2004a) reopened the discussion about the tension between external intervention and local autonomy, calling for proportionate approaches based upon self-evaluation. Significantly, this approach was expressed as a duty to meet community and individual needs, a principle underpinning both the emerging *Curriculum for Excellence* and Scotland's approach to education for citizenship:

> Delivering excellence in education requires both professional freedom and public accountability. Scotland already has a

world renowned system of inspection and evaluation: we will build on this to ensure further, sustained improvement in our schools. We need systems that are proportionate, that focus on outcomes, that promote self-evaluation, and that provide targeted support to those who are struggling. We will focus the role of the Scottish Executive on the national framework to ensure that Scotland performs well, that we stand comparison with other high performing nations, and that we improve our performance over time. We will expect local authorities to drive improvement at the local level and to add value to the work of their schools. We will expect schools to meet the needs of their community and each and every one of their pupils. We will act to build, at each level, systems of tough, intelligent accountability that foster ambition and allow proper, informed public scrutiny. (Scottish Executive, 2004a: p. 6)

The relationship between the national accountability framework and the development of education for citizenship in Scotland

The Scottish understanding of citizenship education continues to be developed and interpreted. Of equal importance is the issue of coverage and the extent to which citizenship receives consistent, planned attention across and within every school. In a system with minimal curriculum prescription, the keys to achieving this ambition are national guidance and support aimed at building consensus about the relative importance of citizenship education. In Scotland an LTS discussion paper, *Education for Citizenship* (Learning and Teaching Scotland, 2002) provided a rationale. This continues to command broad agreement:

One of the intentions of education for citizenship is to encourage the development by pupils of personal values and an increasing awareness, as they mature, of widely held social values. Values education is a complex and challenging area in which the contribution of the school sits alongside many other influences, including those of the family and the wider community. However, it is a basic tenet of the Scottish approach to

> citizenship education that the school can play an important role in developing personal values, political, social, environmental and spiritual – through the experiences it offers and through sustained emphasis on responsible behaviour and concern for others. (HMIE, 2006a: p. 3)

The overall goal of citizenship education is 'development of capability for thoughtful and responsible participation in political, economic, social and cultural life' (LTS, 2002: p. 5).

Since the publication of *Education for Citizenship*, the development of *Curriculum for Excellence* has led to a more fully articulated expression of educational purpose and, importantly, a framework for development. The 2002 citizenship paper describes four *learning outcomes*:

- knowledge and understanding;
- skills and competences;
- values and dispositions;
- creativity and enterprise.

These draw on an earlier LTS paper *Teaching for Effective Learning* (Learning and Teaching Scotland, 1996) and they foreshadow elements of the statements of *Experiences and Outcomes* (Learning and Teaching Scotland, 2009) published to support *Curriculum for Excellence*.

Like *Curriculum for Excellence*, education for citizenship is more readily understood as curriculum rationale, not a series of curricular components. However, those responsible for measuring accountability and reporting on progress become the arbiters of quality, defining expectations about practice and performance through what they choose to praise or censure. The subtitle of the HMIE 2006a report on education for citizenship, *A Portrait of Current Practice in Scottish Schools and Pre-school Centres*, denotes the need to describe rather than define features of effective practice. The lack of prescription associated with the developing *Curriculum for Excellence* risks the possibility of sometimes undesirable variability within and across schools. Where outcomes are difficult to measure, there is a tendency for evaluators, whether internal or external, to commentate rather than evaluate.

As a permeating feature of the curriculum, education for citizenship is difficult to define and exemplify. The key questions are about:

- Responsibility for delivery, where, by whom and in what ways will education for citizenship be delivered?
- Consensus about quality and effective practice, what measures will be used and who will apply them?
- Competing demands on time within the curriculum, how should education for citizenship be prioritised amongst competing curriculum themes or 'subjects', and within the wider, public expectations about the transformative capacity of schools?

Cross-cutting or whole-school themes are generally seen to be the responsibility of all involved with the direct delivery of learning and teaching. The Bullock Report (Bullock, 1975) for example, argued strongly for the concept of every teacher as a teacher of language. This principle resonates with the concept within *Curriculum for Excellence* of three cross-cutting themes which are 'the responsibility of all practitioners', defined as 'health and wellbeing', 'literacy' and 'numeracy'. The most cursory review of the experiences and outcomes supporting each of the three themes shows that neither individually nor collectively do they encompass all that citizenship is about. Education for citizenship has to be the concern and the responsibility of the school and its wider community, underpinned by a commitment to inclusion.

Encompassing such complexity strains traditional accountability models which tend to focus on scrutinising and evaluating inputs by staff and outputs in the form of data, first-hand testimony, perceptions and observed practice and experience. However, aspects of the curriculum that are associated with relatively hard measures of performance tend to be regarded as being of higher relative importance. Literacy and numeracy and courses which lead to formal certification, tend to have primacy over 'lower-stakes' themes, creating a curricular hierarchy of esteem. Within this hierarchy, high-status subjects are timetabled often on a daily basis. In contrast, citizenship education is sometimes calendared rather than embedded.

Designing and applying an accountability model for education for citizenship is challenging. Unravelling the contributions schools make to promoting inclusion, engagement and participation within and across their communities is particularly difficult for an outside evaluator, although the prevailing ethos in a school is an important indicator. Furthermore, there is an inherent paradox in any individual or body external to the learning community holding that community to account for the quality of its provision for education for citizenship. At the heart of effective education for citizenship is the principle that the most effective context within which young people can learn about participation and engagement is one which is participatory and engaging, modelling a self-determining and democratic society. The need for the intervention of an outside body could appear to be anathema to effective citizenship education. The *necessity* for any outside moderation of the quality of citizenship education in a learning community would seem to indicate that community's capacity to be self-determining and genuinely self-evaluative was relatively undeveloped. This applies as much at national and education authority levels as it does to individual schools. As HMIE describe it:

> All pupils' learning progresses in an atmosphere characterised by respect for individual learners and their communities. By being a microcosm of good citizenship, schools and early education establishments can instil a sense of purpose in young people that will give them confidence to participate actively in society. (HMIE, 2006a: p. 14)

And that cannot be inspected.

Over time, HMIE reports on education for citizenship suggest a development in expectations. HMIE often use the metaphor of 'raising the bar' to describe this phenomenon. The HMIE 2003 *Taking a Closer Look at Citizenship* series build explicitly upon the key elements outlined in the 2002 LTS paper and the associated audit materials for the pre-school, primary and secondary school stages. Given the enabling rhetoric, the tone of these materials is surprisingly directive: 'Use of the audit materials will precede use of the self-evaluation guide, which is designed to help you to evaluate the quality of provision (HMIE: 2003: p. 3).'

By 2005 expectations had developed sufficiently to the extent that when highlighting areas of relative weakness in national provision, HMIE (2006b: p. 2) highlighted 'the need for a clearer and more consistent approach to Education for Citizenship'. In 2009 the Senior Chief Inspector, reflecting on earlier weaknesses in provision, reported himself 'encouraged' by recent national strategic frameworks, but cautioned that 'the challenge remains ... to translate aspiration to action' (HMIE, 2009: p. 1).

The desired improvements in learners' whole-school experience remain elusive, although HMIE do report improvements in the leadership of education for citizenship, underlining the earlier HMIE 2002 assessment that:

> The curriculum alone will not develop good citizens … the citizens of tomorrow will develop most effectively in a vibrant school community that is rooted in openness and mutual trust … [with] strong links with parents, the broader community and society at large, both nationally and internationally. (HMIE, 2002: p. 2)

Early HMIE reports on citizenship education contain more exhortation than exemplification, with limited detail about how desirable features of leadership, well-geared establishments and ambient social and educational conditions work in synergy to support the achievement of effective education for citizenship. Latterly, materials produced within the *Journey to Excellence* (HMIE, 2007b) series included more commentary on practice seen to be effective in supporting effective citizenship education.

Looking ahead: evaluating delivery of citizenship education

> Policy-makers should be sufficiently open-minded to consider the accountability system in its entirety and ask whether it is effectively fulfilling the goals that have been set to it. In doing so, they need to ask fundamental questions … about the effect their regime is having on the teaching profession. (Assessment Reform Group, 2009: p. 19)

To ensure the sustained, effective delivery of *Curriculum for Excellence*, and within that the development of citizenship, there is a need to develop further the web of responsibility. What is required is continuous and progressive action and interaction among:

- children, young people, families and the wider community (citizens);
- local and national governments, including policy makers (government);

- providers, including frontline providers and managers (providers).

These groups need to work and learn within a culture wherein national and local approaches, including those relating to scrutiny or accountability, are founded on a shared commitment to improve provision for learners.

Curriculum for Excellence recognises the tensions for schools in making the curriculum meaningful and relevant for each learner while delivering across a broad range of expectations and priorities. HMIE have a role to play in giving greater prominence to issues, approaches, themes and subjects which might not be regarded as priorities by schools, authorities or parent bodies. This includes explicit and focused attention to citizenship education. This is power to influence rather than command; where HMIE inspect and report on an aspect of provision, schools and education authorities tend to pay attention.

Citizenship education is embedded across the experiences and outcomes of *Curriculum for Excellence*. It is also explicit not only in the four capacities, but also within the theme of Health and Wellbeing:

> Everyone within each learning community, whatever their contact with children and young people may be, shares the responsibility for creating a positive ethos and climate of respect and trust – one in which everyone can make a positive contribution to the wellbeing of each individual within the school community. (Learning and Teaching Scotland, 2009: p. 2)

There are clear links between the approaches proposed in 2002 for the delivery of effective citizenship education and the advice supporting the development of *Curriculum for Excellence* (Learning and Teaching Scotland, 2006–10), including:

- participation by learners in decision-making;
- development of authentic community links;
- active approaches to learning, including discussion, debate and investigation;
- whole-school activities that raise issues of citizenship issues, ethical decision-making and shared values.

As the statutory roles of the successor body to HMIE, Education Scotland, and of education authorities continue to be refocused in relation to quality improvement in schools, there remains a strong commitment to and support for self-evaluation. This self-evaluative approach has been championed more widely across public services in Scotland. Although still at an early stage, the development of coherent, local approaches to cross-service quality improvement by practitioners, including schools, has the potential to deliver more immediate, democratic accountability to local communities. Evaluations of individual elements of public service provision run the risk of missing the bigger contextual picture.

This emergent, multi-agency approach to scrutiny of the impact of public services is well matched to the promotion of effective education for citizenship. It also addresses concerns about the impact of serial external scrutiny directed towards assuring accountability for public services. These concerns led to the establishment of the Crerar Review (Crerar, 2007) which signalled the possibility of a new direction for external scrutiny, with greater synergy of the work of those scrutinising the work of public bodies: 'Given a new core purpose to provide independent assurance within a wider performance management and reporting framework, the various functions of external scrutiny and the organisations responsible for carrying them out should now operate effectively together' (Crerar, 2007: p. 6). Crerar also suggested a need for more trust, resonating with the philosophy underpinning *Curriculum for Excellence*: 'The main thrust of our conclusions is that, if the workload created by scrutiny is to be reduced, Ministers and the Parliament will need to "let go". This will require a new approach to the identification of a response to risk...' (Crerar, 2007: p. 58).

Effective education for citizenship is difficult to inspect. Schools which demonstrate the qualities required to develop citizenship are also largely self-sustaining in their capacity to deliver it. Effective teachers and school leaders need to feel themselves accountable, first to their children, young people and families. Both HMIE and managing authorities have a role in ensuring education for citizenship is on every school's agenda, but prescription of practice will not lead to real change.

Education for citizenship is a long-term investment and its full impact is measurable only as one of the most lagging of indicators. However, the establishment of an ethos of mutuality within and across schools can have immediate *measurable* benefits. These are most evident in terms of relationships within an institution and, in turn, on learning, teaching and outcomes for children and young people. Measuring these qualitative improvements needs engagement over time and improved processes, and better approaches to evaluation and evidence-gathering, which in turn brings into question the leadership and ownership of quality improvement processes.

There is a continuing debate (Murtagh, 2010) nationally about the relative roles of HMIE and education authorities in relation to quality assurance. Recent calls for reform appear to be related less to issues of governance and more to questions about the targeting of inspection and its relationship with school support (Munro, 2010). If regulation and guidance are to be relaxed in favour of school autonomy and creativity, is there a compelling need to have external evaluators?

In a paper describing international approaches to improving quality of education at a national level through the use of a strong public accountability model, Digby Swift (2008) argues for an approach 'building on shared accountability and wider systems of quality assurance'. He suggests that Scotland's approach, one which emphasises 'systems of self-evaluation—internal accountability—as a means of quality control' might readily and usefully be adopted elsewhere as a driver for improvement, particularly in low income countries where it is likely to be more effective than 'market-based' schemes.

One of the challenges of a development as comprehensive as *Curriculum for Excellence* is that of matching its repercussions and scope to a school's capacity for curriculum planning and development. Earlier curriculum reforms in Scotland have been less wholesale and more stage- or theme-related. However, curriculum reform often brings with it a call for wider reform. *Curriculum for Excellence* is associated with calls for reforms in various areas, including:

- the way HMIE discharges its role (Munro, 2010);
- local government control of education;
- leadership development and CPD for teachers (Learning and Teaching Scotland, 2011);
- teacher education (Donaldson, 2011);
- accreditation of teachers' qualifications (Buie, 2010);
- certification of learners' experiences (Learning and Teaching Scotland, 2011).

It is difficult to strike an appropriate balance between the freedom that teachers and schools have under *Curriculum for Excellence* to vary the learning approaches they adopt, including the content they cover, and to deliver society's wider expectations of the socialising effect of schooling. In a mature system where schools engaged effectively with stakeholders, and communities were self-evaluative and had the capacity and capability to reflect and improve, there would be little need for long-route accountability to maintain this balance.

At the current stage of the development of *Curriculum for Excellence* greater clarity and detail is required beyond the broad purposes and outcomes of education. There is a need to develop a better understanding and some consensus about the standards children and young people will be expected to achieve and the means by which long-term outcomes are to be assured. This will require better approaches to assessing learners' performance and the quality of their experiences. To avoid the negative influence of external accountability, robust self-evaluation is required which is capable of assuring key stakeholders of the quality of the establishment's work, drawing on valid and reliable data on performance which commands public confidence. As external evaluators adopt an increasingly participative approach, schools will be more appropriately, rather than less, accountable.

The future of education for citizenship in Scotland is inextricably linked to the success of *Curriculum for Excellence*. While external evaluators from local and national government can measure participation and engagement, the true test of the success of that initiative will be the long-term outcomes for children and young people. The current repositioning of the roles and responsibilities of those charged with monitoring education in Scotland is an opportunity to recast the web of accountabilities more closely aligned to the interests of learners and families.

Developing Outward-Facing Schools
Where Citizenship is a Lived Experience

Alison Peacock

Accountability

If we are to be held to account as school leaders, then let us be judged first and foremost on the quality of our children as citizens. Let us be held to account for the way our children view learning, for their level of interest, for their self-belief, their sense of community, their optimism that the future is theirs for the making. In English primary schools the standards agenda has, without doubt, made school leaders accountable. However, the pressure of high-stakes testing has distorted the education that we offer. Values and principles about the core purposes of education have become suppressed in favour of adherence to teaching that focuses on measurable outcomes.

The notion of accountability within English primary schools has dominated the agenda increasingly since the 1988 Education Act. As the Association of Teachers and Lecturers state in their policy document 'New accountability for schools' (2010) there is no longer a debate about whether teachers *should* be accountable but 'the questions are to whom and how?' As the headteacher of an English primary school, I am more than aware of the constant pressure of accountability. Headteachers are accountable to a wide range of stakeholders that include children, parents, staff, governors, local authority inspectors, Ofsted and the Department for Education. Depressingly, this 'top–down' model leads many teachers to pressurise their class of children in the name of 'standards'. Parents seek additional tuition outside school; all around us is the worry of test performance and ranking. Even when we self-evaluate school performance, too often the measures that we use are dominated by pupil performance within the core curriculum areas of maths and English. This has led to a culture of fear in many schools where measurable outcomes, in terms of test results, dominate the primary curriculum. School league tables, safeguarding regulations and the constant prospect of a phone call from Ofsted, are enough to send a shiver down the spine of the bravest school leader.

In this chapter, I argue that as a profession we should indeed be accountable. However, let us make sure that we are aiming for the most salient outcomes. There can be no more important responsibility within our schools than building generations of young people who have a genuine sense of agency within society.

To achieve this we need to provide school communities that provide real-life, authentic, examples of what it is to exist within a democracy driven by values and principles. Throughout I shall refer to the practice that we have developed at The Wroxham School. As a headteacher, I believe passionately in the importance of a principled approach to school leadership. The following description of our school is intended as a basis for contextual understanding of how citizenship education can be realised as an intrinsic part of everyday experience. It is not something that is planned for separately, but is more a way of being.

A principled approach to school improvement

When I joined as headteacher in January 2003, the school was in the Ofsted category of special measures. Having previously been described by an inspector as 'unteachable' in 2001, stringent behaviour management systems had rendered the children almost totally passive within classrooms. No one asked questions, no one volunteered, no one showed any interest; because to do so was to risk being labelled a swot or 'boffin' by your peers. The overriding classroom culture at that time was one of apathy, boredom and disenfranchisement. On the playground, however, all the frustrations of the day spilled out. Bullying was commonplace, fights broke out regularly and for many children conflict at lunchtime ruined any prospect of learning in the afternoon. As a newly appointed headteacher my aim was to inspire the school community to believe in the prospect of a bright positive future. For two years Her Majesty's Inspectors (HMI) had noted limited progress. What was needed was not more of the same, but a new way forward built on the notion that learning can be magical and irresistible if we find the right opportunities. I was convinced that we needed to swim against the tide of school improvement that measures progress through setting tightly defined targets. What was needed was hope, the art of the possible, a sense of optimism.

I began by telling the children, staff and parents that we were going to become known as a 'listening school'. The message was that our learning journey as a school community was going to be a collective endeavour. I made it clear from the earliest days that the best answers often lead to new questions and that our journey of improvement would be exciting, shaped by dialogue between all participants. Our journey would be based on working together to create exciting learning opportunities that would mean none of us would be able to wait to get to school each morning. However, the curriculum followed by the school at this time was rigidly timetabled and monitored through observations, planning scrutiny and summative analysis of child and adult performance. Subjects were planned using national schemes of work and there was little confidence for crea-tivity. We set about enlivening the children's interest in learning by invit-ing a wide range of visitors into school. We worked with artists, a poet, musicians, scientists, a youth rock band—anyone who could bring learn-ing to life. Gradually the atmosphere around the school began to change. Children began to get excited about learning almost in spite of themselves and teachers appreciated a fresh approach to curriculum monitoring which was based on celebration rather than criticism. Our alternative approach to school improvement based on the principles of trust, co-agency and inclusion, rapidly enabled us to be taken off special measures and within three years to be judged by Ofsted to be outstanding (Ofsted, 2006; 2009). The story of our development has been co-researched by the University of Cambridge and will be documented in a forthcoming book entitled *Creating Learning without Limits* (Swann *et al.* 2012: forthcoming).

Giving adults and children a voice

Our progress had been achieved so rapidly because the aims of citizenship education underpinned every decision that we took. We became inspired to learn and to challenge ourselves because everyone was given a voice; everyone's views were listened to and respected. Decisions were made and evaluated collectively.

In my previous school I had participated in an Economic and Social Research Council (ESRC) funded research project into student voice

(Fielding and Bragg, 2003) and had initiated the practice of whole-school mixed-age meeting groups. This radical democratic process forms an alternative to the model of a school council, enabling the whole community to participate in discussion, debate and decision-making. When I arrived at Wroxham School there was no school council. Indeed no one within the school, adult or child, had a voice; decisions were taken on their behalf by local authority advisers and the outcomes were inspected each term by Her Majesty's Inspectors. On my first day of headship I held a circle time with each class and their teacher. This meeting was a way of getting to know the children, but crucially it gave the message that we were all going to be involved in finding out what our school was good at, in order that we could improve still further. By March 2003 we had implemented the circle meetings that still take place each week. These mixed-age meetings take place in each classroom from Years 1–6, with another group in the hall and another in the staffroom. The meeting lasts for 15 minutes and is followed by playtime. Initially, each group was led by a teacher using an outline session plan written by me with ideas for warm up and warm down games, news of the week ahead and a focus for discussion and feedback. However, by September 2003, it was agreed that the Year 6 children would be confident enough to take the lead. The meetings continue in this format and provide a forum for whole school participation. Issues discussed are initiated by children, staff, governors or a mixture of all three. Decisions are often quite small because the groups meet so regularly. This form of regular dialogue ensures that communication is effective and that decisions taken are effectively evaluated. Crucially, discussion leads to action and dialogue leads to empathy.

In preparation for the seminar paper that is the basis of this chapter, I asked two children that I came across in the library, to tell me what circle meetings were for. Alice (aged 10) commented: 'I think we have circle meetings to discuss what goes on in school, so everyone knows about it and it's not secret … We discuss things and we work as a team … the Haiti fair and discussions like that'. I asked her who decides what action is taken: 'We all decide as a group and we have votes and everyone gets their share of their ideas.'

Megan (aged 8) said the meetings were held 'so that people know how you feel'. She went on to say that it was an opportunity 'to talk about things you're upset about', the benefit of mixed age groups being that 'you might already know your class's ideas'.

Without the meetings, Megan pondered, 'you wouldn't really know how other people feel and the teachers wouldn't know how to sort it out'.

Whose voices are heard?

Sir Al Aynsely-Green, Children's Commissioner for England (2005–9), commented in the *Times Educational Supplement* (Maddem 2009) that 'children only tell teachers what they think they want to hear'. His argument was that a 'crisis' has been caused by the 'constant obligation' for teachers to consult with children and to record evidence of doing so for Ofsted. The Children's Commissioner was calling for an improvement in communication between adults and children, apparently recognising that consultation is often seriously flawed. The real danger to citizenship education is that our children see through the adults' agenda of consultation and instead experience a model of participation that is tokenistic (Taylor and Robinson, 2009). Experiences such as this throughout school life ultimately reinforce feelings of powerlessness within society. Accountability to the aims of citizenship education means providing a principled, living model of democracy that enables empowerment within individual school settings. We cannot afford for our teaching to be undermined by day-to-day experiences that go against the values we discuss in the classroom. Small actions count. There are many schools that proudly display vision statements about equality, but are places, nonetheless, where it is deemed entirely acceptable for adults to push into the dinner queue.

A school culture, however, that runs on democratic principles means that all participants feel able to contribute meaningfully. Open dialogue between adults and children builds a partnership approach to learning and assessment built on shared understanding and trust. Trust is crucially important. Emma (aged 10) talking to school visitors about assessment confided that she had to think hard about how honest she should be in her self-assessment book as there were consequences to letting the teacher know if you did not understand something. She trusted her teacher, however, and knew that her learning would be supported by being honest in her feedback. The implication of this revelation is clear. Assessment feedback from children is only as good as the relationship that exists between teacher and pupil (Leitch *et al.*, 2006). Similarly, children quickly learn in many classrooms that to question the teacher's knowledge or to suggest that an area of subject content has already been covered is to risk reprimand. Children learn the rhetoric of consultation that pleases their teachers and also the 'no go' territory that is not considered respectful even if this directly concerns their own learning and progress.

It should be obvious that it is not enough to talk to our young people about the importance of democratic values and the principles of citizenship education. They need to *experience* these values and principles in action. The irony here is that we have generations of teachers and children who have experienced anything but autonomy within classrooms. At a recent conference I was explaining to a colleague my reservations about school council meetings in some schools where all the important issues have been prejudged and decided before the agenda is even written. Her response was that in her school, staff meetings had a very similar feel. Management brought forward an item for 'discussion' and then announced what the solution was going to be. I had never equated the notion of teacher dis-empowerment so closely with the children's experience before and the parallel was stark.

Enabling teachers

The report of the Cambridge Primary Review (Alexander, 2009: p. 3) calls for 'a pedagogy of evidence and principle' where teachers would be informed by 'repertoire rather than recipe and of principle rather than pre-scription', with teaching and learning 'properly informed by research'. This plea for 'greater professional flexibility and creativity' refers to the appar-ent powerlessness of a profession that has been buffeted by the political agenda. Teachers with no sense of agency cannot be expected to teach effectively and can certainly not be expected to approach citizenship edu-cation with conviction. School leaders need to enable teachers to regain the energy and purpose to develop their practice through rich enquiry-based professional development without predetermined outcomes.

Resisting ability labelling

At Wroxham we have a whole-school approach to teaching without ability labelling. We refuse to accept the doctrine of 'gifted and talented' and 'special needs' which leads to practice that ranks children one against another. Neither do we accept that children are intrinsically 'lazy' or 'demotivated'. Our approach builds on the research that I participated in for the ground-breaking study *Learning Without Limits* (Hart *et al.*, 2004). We work together to find opportunities for each individual child to access learning in a meaningful way. This is not always easy and there are times when we struggle to hold onto this ethos. However, the rewards are great. Children who may be 'written off' in another environment, families who would otherwise feel alienated by school, are able to contribute to our community in the way that suits them best. This ethos responds to the individual needs of each child and adult. Our school ethos is built on the idea that children all too easily become defined by the labels that they are given. If we believe that we have a culture where each individual is free to talk about their learning, it follows that the individual learner needs to experience freedom to make choices about how much challenge they can cope with within each lesson. Typically, within each lesson there will be opportunities for children to make decisions about the next steps in their learning. A range of tasks with varying degrees of difficulty are planned by the teacher, but it is the child who decides where she or he begins and the task that she or he will attempt first.

This is not a soft option, but an approach that relies on co-agency and trust. It follows that if we believe children have a right to participate as citizens within the society of school they have the right to contribute directly to decisions that affect their learning. Too often citizenship education is theoretical and fails to build on actual lived experience. If we believe in pupil voice as a concept we should apply this to all aspects of school life. In fact, it is far more important that individual children can engage in meaningful dialogue about their learning than it is that they have the option to vote for play equipment on the playground or the colour of new paint in the toilets.

Choice and independence

An important aspect of citizenship education is learning to make informed choices. If school presents as a place where compliance and uniformity is the dominant culture, our children, parents and staff are given little room to exercise choice. The traditions of power and control within many institutions run counter to the current requirement by Ofsted to demonstrate community and family involvement.

Independence can be built from the very earliest days in nursery. In our school, children and families are invited to visit prior to taking up their nursery place. Each child who is allocated a place is sent a personal letter in the post welcoming them to their new school. For some children, this may be the first letter they have ever received that is addressed personally to them. One parent told me that her son was so excited to receive a letter from his new school that he insisted on sending back a reply, painstakingly drawing a picture even though mark making was not normally a chosen area of interest. His reply is still on my office wall.

The independence and encouragement of individuality that begins in the foundation stage is built upon throughout the rest of the school. The sense of being part of a group is an important part of learning that takes place in those early days. Children learn to play alongside and with others in harmony. They learn that the resources are available every day but need to be tidied away carefully in order that they can be easily accessed the next day. These are not rules for the sake of rules, but a code for living alongside one another comfortably and safely. Families also learn that they are welcome in school and that their concerns are never too trivial and will be taken seriously.

As our curriculum has developed, we have become increasingly adept at building on shared ideas both within classes, across and beyond the school. Our website www.wroxham.herts.sch.uk is constructed around class blogs where videos, photographs and comments are displayed. This has meant that school-based learning experiences can be shared with families in a very accessible way. Recently, I was asking a child in Year 1 about his transition to his new class. He told me that he used the blog at home with his mummy and sister so that they could know what his new class would be like. Although the classrooms are next door to each other, the virtual experience of exploring the next year group offered reassuring opportunities to see the kinds of learning that he might experience next.

Children who maintain intrinsic motivation to learn are a joy to work with. We have found that by offering a thematic curriculum and by offering children real choices and control within that structure, there has been a dramatic movement away from 'boffin' labels to one where it is 'cool' to challenge yourself.

Dealing with real-life issues

Understanding of society and community should lead to debate about issues such as inequality, class, gender, poverty and privilege, environmental sustainability, status and compliance. These are big ideas with no easy answers. Indeed, this is the reason that education for citizenship is so important. We have to approach this aspect of curriculum with an open mind. Our children and young people need to recognise that the dilemmas the modern world faces are real and important. If we believe that future generations can make a positive difference, we have to empower our children to experience this as a reality. They need to experience democracy first hand and be encouraged to engage with authentic issues which they can attempt to resolve.

A collective response

Aspects of community such as being moved to tears by a beautiful piece of performance poetry or feeling compelled to rise to your feet as part of a standing ovation, remind us what it is to share an experience with other human beings. When I first joined Wroxham School the children and staff had been pitched one against another in an attempt to force school improvement. This model of change focuses on blame, with individual performance mattering more than collective achievement. It is a school-improvement model that requires individual adults and children to recognise their faults and work towards measurable targets and levels. The premise is that if someone else points out your faults you are more likely to work hard to redress them. An alternative approach builds on enabling individuals to engage in dialogue that recognizes their successes, in order that they are inspired to challenge themselves to take the next steps in partnership with others.

Schools, by definition, are living examples of community. We need to ensure that the example we offer is one where diversity is celebrated and where genuine partnership is built from mutual respect amongst *all* participants. This means working hard to embrace difference rather than seeking to suppress it. It means giving recognition to the importance of surprise, the necessity for us to continually change, to develop, to innovate. Learning is a continuous process and should always be open to new ideas; consequently our schools should also be fluid, dynamic organisations that rely on creativity as their central construct, rather than tradition.

Assessment as a collaborative process

Assessment at our school is a deeply embedded process. Children make informed decisions related to a wide range of activities and tasks throughout each day. As they move through the school they become increasingly articulate about their learning in each area of the curriculum because they are encouraged to self-assess and review as part of the process of choosing levels of work and task. They know that to make a mistake or to change your mind should be viewed as an essential part of learning. They also know that they will always be given the option of attempting work, reviewing progress and then switching either to something with more challenge or to a task that enables consolidation, prior to moving on. This ethos enables all individuals to gain control over their learning and to work towards self-imposed challenges. As a school we aim to sweep away the complacency that comes with seeing 'ability' as fixed. Our anti-determinist approach aims to encourage every individual, both child and adult, to build capacity in all aspects of learning, thus dispelling the notion of intelligence as an innate fixed commodity. The resulting self-knowledge and confidence enables our learners to engage in assessment with a 'growth mind set' (Dweck, 2007).

We hold termly family consultation meetings which are led by the child. Our aim is to provide the child with an opportunity to share aspects of their learning where they are proud of their achievements, to talk about future challenges and to engage in a dialogue about how best they can overcome hurdles with the support of parents and teachers. The dialogue usually focuses on reflective notes that the child has made, accompanied by examples of work that she has chosen to share. Recently, our Year 4 children introduced the innovation of creating a montage of photographs to present their recent learning. I join these meetings in Years 5 and 6 and help to ensure that all decisions or ideas that we jointly discuss are recorded and acted upon. These meetings are all about learning and are not about attainment. Interestingly, at our most recent Year 6 review day only one parent asked about Standard Attainment Tests (SATs) and national curriculum levels. Our experience has been that families are primarily interested whether their child is happy, challenged and fulfilled. The agenda of ranking one child against another has been eradicated from our dialogue with families. This liberates us to talk about individuals within a supportive community instead of individuals pitched one against another for survival.

For several years we have produced written reports in the summer term that have been created in partnership between each child and their teacher. These reports are written electronically from Year 1 upwards and take the form of a written dialogue. Younger children buddy with older peers from elsewhere in the school to compose their comments. The child's comments are then built on by the teacher responding directly with suggestions for new learning and reminders of other successes achieved throughout the year. The reports come to me for additional comment and are also added to by the family. Subsequently, each child's self-assessment for the core subjects together with parental response and any other particularly insightful reflection is reviewed by me. I then cut and paste the comments onto new record sheets for each individual as a summative record, with added curriculum levels and targets for the new teaching team who will work with the child from September. It is important to emphasise that asking the child to reflect on her learning is only one part of the process; following up her comments, the teacher's comments and those of the family, with planned actions, make the process authentic and worthwhile for all involved. This rigorous dialogic approach enables assessment to be continuous and genuine.

Some teachers provide children with self-assessment journals which are confidential between teaching team and child. Others set up individual blogs so that children can upload examples of their work to share with their family at home (this is particularly valuable where some family members no longer see the child very regularly).

Other opportunities for assessment may take place following group learning, some assessment takes place in test conditions. The key to validity is to provide continual opportunity for open honest dialogue and review and to ensure that children recognise assessment as an ongoing process rather than a goal to achieve and metaphorically collapse against once it has been reached.

Accountability to Ofsted

The priorities of Ofsted have the capacity to wield tremendous influence within schools. It is therefore highly welcome that the inspection framework (Ofsted, 2009) places a continuous, insistent, emphasis on a wide range of outcomes that can only be judged to be 'outstanding' if the school experience is lived as a participative outward-facing community. Schools are currently specifically graded on 'the extent to which pupils contribute to the school and wider community' (Ofsted, 2009: p. 13), their effective promotion of 'community cohesion' (Ofsted, 2009: p. 7), 'the effectiveness with which the school promotes equal opportunity and tackles discrimination' (Ofsted, 2009: p. 14) and their partnership approach. These outcomes explicitly require the school to demonstrate the effectiveness of their approach to citizenship. However, the Ofsted framework is being revised for implementation from 2012. We have to hope that their focus on these areas continues to be a priority.

Ofsted (2010) published a report into the nature of citizenship education in schools. As part of this survey, 23 primary schools were inspected. The report concludes that it is easier to 'incorporate aspects of citizenship into their curricula and the life of the school' (Ofsted 2010: p. 40) in primary schools than it is in many secondary settings. They found that children generally had good levels of achievement in the area of rights and responsibilities, the environment and sustainability, globalisation and interdependence. However, there were often gaps in children's knowledge about local and national democratic institutions and world politics as portrayed by the media. Skills such as discussion and debate were found to be strengths in many of the schools visited. In terms of pupil voice, primary children were generally offered greater opportunities: 'the responsibilities given to pupils and the school council were more substantial than in some of the secondary schools visited' (Ofsted 2010: p. 42). Areas for improvement reflected the insular nature of many schools. Comment was made that there was 'too little use of local opportunities for pupils to participate in real activities beyond the school' (Ofsted 2010: p. 44) and none of the schools visited liaised with secondary schools about citizenship.

Leadership for social justice

Politicians increasingly look to schools as agents of social change. According to Theoharis (2007), school leaders of the future will need to develop the skills of 'leadership for social justice'. Fullan (2003) similarly describes the 'moral imperative' that is needed 'to make a difference beyond the school'. We need enlightened, supportive schools at the centre of local communities where children and families are inspired to believe in themselves and in their collective power to make a difference.

This vision relies upon an approach to school leadership that is outward facing and enabling. This involves struggle, it involves thinking and debate and a tussle with conscience. If someone who has had significantly different life experiences to the majority of our children joins our school, how should we accept them into our community? Do we allow for their individuality? Do we seek to eradicate difference in the name of cohesion? Or do we have the open-mindedness to enrich our own experience through learning about theirs?

The real challenge then, for school leaders, is to become accountable for curriculum and assessment practice that will enable young citizens to experience success rather than failure. Our children's experience of school should be one where individuality and difference are highly prized, boundaries are broadened and freedom to innovate is celebrated. In other words, schools need to be responsive democratic centres of inspiration providing a model for future society where every individual knows they are valued for who they are. If we can move towards this, we can move towards education for citizenship that will give new generations the creativity and tenacity they need to ensure that the global community has a sustainable future.

Conclusion: Half Full or Half Empty?
The Future of Education for Citizenship

Henry Maitles

Introduction

Education for citizenship in its rights-based context has a relatively short history in British schools. It is 14 years since the Advisory Committee known as the Crick report produced its document, in the light of the election of a Labour Government in 1997 and David Blunkett in charge of education; and 10 years since the Scottish Executive Review Group developed its conclusions for Scotland. This was set against a backdrop of political and constitutional development, including the introduction of the 1998 Human Rights Act, a growing interest in the UN Convention on the Rights of the Child, the establishment of a Scottish Parliament and a Welsh Assembly and the creation of an assembly and elected mayor for London (Osler and Starkey, 2001; Deuchar, 2004; Maitles and Deuchar, 2004). In wider philosophical terms, perhaps the renewed interest in the citizenship agenda has emerged from a more general renewal of interest in values in education and also the perceived need for a more participative approach to school organisation (Ruddock and Flutter, 2004; MacBeath and Moos, 2004; Maitles, 2005). However, one of the ironies of education for citizenship over the last few years is that the attempt to develop a healthy respect for issues such as integrity, honesty, self-sacrifice and compassion is problematic at a time when these very virtues are under critique at the very highest levels of the institutions of the state. If our young people do not perceive our politicians, bankers, police and media as having these qualities, then there are problems for education for citizenship programmes. Further, the experience of the riots in several English cities in the summer of 2011 and the demonisation of young people in their wake means that education for citizenship is both more difficult and more essential.

Over the last decade there has been much good practice and some negative experiences, some of it highlighted in this work. The central thrust of this book asks some of the key questions surrounding education for citizenship: What is education for? What is the role of the school in developing positive attitudes amongst young people? How can controversial issues be raised in the classroom? How do we develop critical citizens? The authors would not claim to give definitive answers, but begin to explore the questions in a way helpful to classroom practitioners. One of the real bonuses of the discussion which took place around education for citizenship was precisely that the focus was on the whole nature of education and exactly what our education system should be trying to develop in young people. But in recent years throughout the world there has been an emphasis on target setting, particularly concentrating on exam results. This has tended to distort the nature of schooling and has meant that the wider issues have been kept in the background; as teachers have concentrated on the exam targets, issues such as citizenship tend to get squeezed from the school day (Davies, 2000; Gillborn and Youdell, 2000; Cowan and Maitles, 2010), despite some welcome rhetoric from government on the importance of citizenship and of instilling a respect for lifelong learning.

The international context of education for citizenship

Citizenship is a compulsory element in most democracies throughout Europe, North America and the Pacific (Crick, 2000a; Osler and Starkey, 2005; Print, 2007; Kiwan, 2008). Research suggests that political education in schools in Western democracies emphasises political institutions, rights and responsibilities of citizens, debates on current issues and moralism in various combinations (Borhaug, 2008). The largest international survey is the International Civic And Citizenship Education Study/International Association for the Evaluation of Educational Achievement (ICCS/IEA) study (Schulz et al., 2010), which involved some 140,000 students (about 14 years of age) and 62,000 teachers in 38 countries. In terms of content areas, the topics that the ICCS countries most frequently nominated as a major emphasis in civic and citizenship education were human rights (25 countries), understanding different cultures and ethnic groups (23 countries), the environment (23 countries), parliamentary and governmental systems (22 countries) and voting and elections (20 countries).

Topics less frequently nominated as a major emphasis were communications studies (14 countries), legal systems and courts (13 countries), the economy and economics (12 countries), regional institutions and organisations (12 countries), and resolving conflict (11 countries). Only five countries nominated voluntary groups as a major emphasis. However, another finding of note is the significant decrease in civic content knowledge scores between 1999 and 2009 in a number of countries that had comparable data from both civic education surveys: only one country had a statistically significant increase in civic content knowledge among lower secondary students over the past decade. This is rather worrying, as the decade was meant to be one permeated by education for citizenship and in that context we might have expected an increase in this kind of knowledge and understanding.

Students were far more likely to report school-based civic participation than involvement in activities or organisations outside of school. On average, across participating countries, 76 % of ICCS students reported having voted in school elections and 61 % reported voluntary participation in music or drama activities. About 40 % of students said that they had been actively involved in debates, taken part in decision-making about how their school was run, taken part in school assembly discussions, or been candidates for class representative or the school parliament. Involvement in groups helping the community and in charity collections was the most frequent form of participation among lower secondary school students across the ICCS countries. On average, about a third of students reported that they had been involved in this way in the past. The extent to which students engaged in these activities across countries varied considerably, which may be due to cultural differences. For example, the percentage of students reporting participation in groups collecting money for a social cause ranged from a very low 8% in Korea to 60% in Belgium (Flemish).

However, a study such as this needs to be tempered with an examination of the specifics of the countries. When we examine the ideas around citizenship and civics in particular countries, then common themes and differences become clearer.

In the USA there is a well-established 'civics programme' in schools with direct instruction about democracy, political institutions, rights and responsibilities. Hahn (1999) and Torney-Purta *et al.* (1999) found that the focus was on facts and vocabulary rather than on controversial issues, and that US youth had a general but not detailed understanding of government and political process. Print (2007) points out that even the most ardent advocates of citizenship education comment that in recent years it has failed in the USA. However, Hahn (1998) refers to the fact that in the USA many teachers make deliberate efforts to have students follow the news and have class discussions, which leads to enhanced student understanding of current affairs and political issues.

Borhaug (2008) describes the timetabled political education national curriculum in Norway, which aims to encourage students to be critical of political and social structures and to learn how they can influence democracy through various forms of political participation. In his study of upper secondary schools he concludes that voting was the most thoroughly taught form of political participation. He describes the importance of the mock elections in schools running in tandem with Norwegian elections where all the political parties send representatives to schools to present their parties' policies to students. Results of the mock elections receive extensive media coverage. However, Borhaug points out that little attention is given to other forms of participation such as pressure groups, petitions, writing to newspapers and direct action. Additionally, issues of human rights, tolerance, freedom of faith and expression were not systematically taught.

Print (2007) points out that Australia's national citizenship education programme with its extensive and well-prepared curriculum materials could at best be described as marginally successful in raising levels of democratic engagement in a country where voting is compulsory. In spite of the programme, 50% of students surveyed in the 2004–7 Youth Electoral Study felt that they lacked the knowledge to understand party politics and key issues.

In England citizenship education has been compulsory, assessed and inspected since 2002. However, authors such as Breslin (2000) and Osler and Starkey (2005) express concerns that assessment and citizenship education do not sit well together. The Crick Report (QCA, 1998) set out three strands—social and moral responsibility, community involvement and political literacy—with learning outcomes in skills, aptitudes, knowledge and understanding for all key stages (QCA, 1998). However, Lister *et al.* (2001) point out that apart from a few exceptions, in general schools have made little contribution to the development of political literacy. Kiwan (2008) highlights the fact that schemes of work to develop participatory skills are not sufficient because they fail to address issues of inequality, which can lead to disempowerment and lack of motivation to participate. A further shortfall is highlighted by Osler and Starkey (2000; 2005), who state that commitment to human rights and the skills for challenging racism, which are essential attributes of a politically literate citizen, are not addressed. Currently, the government is consulting as to whether the subject called Citizenship should be removed from the timetable and a whole-school permeation model adopted, but there are worries that this would lead to citizenship being downgraded in the eyes of students, parents and teachers.

In Wales there is a statutory curriculum of citizenship with clear learning outcomes at key stages with the emphasis that pupils become literate in political and economic realms, for example by Key Stage 3 pupils are expected to understand issues relating to democracy in Wales, know the rights and responsibilities of a young citizen and how representatives are elected and what their roles are (Philips, 2000). In the Republic of Ireland Civic Social and Political Education is a certified subject; there is a similar concept-based subject in Northern Ireland (Hammond and Looney, 2000).

In Scotland, Maitles (2000) points out that with the advent of the Scottish Parliament political education in schools became an important goal for politicians, a point echoed by Learning and Teaching Scotland (2002: p. 6) who state the importance of 'the ability to understand and participate in the democratic process'. In Scotland citizenship is explicit in the 'responsible citizenship' capacity of the *Curriculum for Excellence* (Scottish Executive, 2004b). Knowledge, skills and values are to permeate the curriculum rather than be taught as a separate subject. However, Torney-Purta *et al.* (1999) point to a general dissatisfaction with cross-curricular approaches where citizenship issues are to be discussed by every teacher but are the responsibility of no teacher.

How much can be expected of schools?

Academics and commentators continue to question the motives behind the introduction of citizenship education. Yet, most would agree with

Hahn (1998; 1999) and Print (2007), who believe that it is the responsibility of schools to teach about democracy and prepare students to be effective democratic citizens. Kerr and Cleaver (2004) point out that many teachers view citizenship education as a politically fashioned quick fix. Writing about civic education in Greece, Makrinioti and Solomon (1999) point out that it is vulnerable to political and social conditioning and can be used as a way to promote political propaganda, a point echoed by Hahn (1998). Rooney (2007) takes this issue further urging us to be wary of citizenship education which he states can be viewed as a programme of behaviour modification, and that it is not the responsibility of teachers and schools to solve political and social problems or issues of low voter turnout and political apathy. Indeed, he points out that citizenship education has thus far failed to reconnect young people to the political system or improve participation rates. Several authors (Lister et al., 2001; Whiteley, 2005; Kiwan 2008) highlight the fact that there is no empirical evidence of a direct correlation between citizenship education and formal political participation. Indeed, David Kerr, interviewed by Kiwan (2008), stated that it would be difficult to measure the effect of citizenship education programmes on political participation. However, it could be that citizenship education is still in its relative infancy and not enough evidence is yet available. Nonetheless, it is to be hoped that students who have been through education for citizenship programmes will have the skills to make informed choices in terms of participation or, indeed, whether they wish to participate.

Whiteley (2005) points out that the expected improvement in civic engagement with the introduction of citizenship education is offset by other factors including the widespread feeling that governments do not deliver on promises—and this was prior to the UK parliamentary expense scandal and issues surrounding the Conservative/Liberal Coalition government. There are many factors outwith the school that influence political engagement, such as the influence of family and peer group (Kennedy, 2007). Political engagement and efficacy is also dependent on levels of education, intelligence, exposure to media, socio-economic class and the hidden curriculum of the school (Hahn, 1998; Torney-Purta et al., 1999; Lister et al., 2001; Kerr et al., 2004; Whiteley, 2005; Print, 2007; Kiwan, 2008).

Further, whilst there is general agreement as to the desire to have a politically aware citizenry, it must be noted that there is no universal agreement as to the value of citizenship, political literacy, activism or pupil voice in schools per se (Lundy, 2007; Whitty and Wisby, 2007; Thornberg, 2008). Rooney (2007), for example, argues that to believe that these kinds of initiatives can be developed in the current UK school system undermines the very nature of education and makes teachers responsible for the ills of society.

Single-issue politics and young people

One of the main drivers behind the introduction of education for citizenship is the perceived lack of interest and involvement of young people in public and political life (Kerr and Cleaver, 2004; Benton *et al.*, 2008) and low election turnout figures for 18–24 year olds (Maitles, 2005; Rooney, 2007; Kiwan, 2008). Another factor is the fear for the state of democracy and the decline in trust of politicians and institution of government (Whiteley, 2005). However, rising engagement with single-issue politics such as the Iraq and Afghanistan wars, world poverty, environmental and animal welfare issues, would appear to suggest that young people in Western democracies, although alienated from formal politics and voting, are active and interested in single-issue campaigning politics where they can see results from their actions (Hahn, 1998; Torney-Purta *et al.*, 1999; Lister *et al.*, 2001; Maitles, 2005). Kiwan (2008) cites research by Pattie in 2004, which found that individualistic participation is common, challenging assertions that people are politically apathetic. Many schools have responded to this through the establishment of eco-schools committees, fair trade groups and a focus on development education programmes. However, media images in a global age also allow children to become exposed to many more controversial social, political and humanitarian issues than ever before, and evidence has illustrated that pupils are keen to discuss such issues and that a programme on citizenship education needs to respond to this (Maitles and Deuchar, 2004). Indeed, the events organised in July 2005 in connection with the 'Make Poverty History' campaign have led to many primary- and secondary-aged pupils becoming actively engaged in community fundraising and awareness campaigns around the alleviation and elimination of poverty in the developing world. Some schools have established forums to respond to pupils' strong views about the need to wage a war against poverty and to enable them to reflect critically upon social and political developments in the media (Deuchar, 2004).

Indeed, although a positive driver towards education for citizenship stems from attempts to promote democratic citizenship, human and participation rights at local, national and global level rights are enshrined in international conventions such as the United Nations Rights of the Child and in the Human Rights Act (Osler and Starkey, 2000b; Spencer, 2000; Verhellen, 2000; Kerr and Cleaver, 2004; Benton *et al.*, 2008). Additionally, there are concerns that democracies have invested more resources into education while experiencing a decline in participation, and there is a logic that better-educated people might be more distrustful of politicians and decide not to vote or to join political parties (Rooney, 2007). Further, we must be aware that many schools see charity activities per se as a way of developing global citizenship. And even within this, there can be a lack of any understanding as to how the money is used and rarely any discussion around the causes of poverty. Holden and Minty (2011), in their study of some 200 school students in England, found that the students could name a charity or discuss charity work or eco-logical work they had been involved in, but had little understanding of the broader issues, such as the complex reasons behind world problems. Indeed, young people saw this as the key element which schools encour-aged in terms of citizenship; nearly all discussions were on personal choice (fair trade, no littering) rather than any meaningful discussion on poverty or wider ecological issues.

Democracy and pupil rights

Inside the school, there is the thorny issue of whether one only learns about democracy rather than living it. If we take the 'living' model, then there are implications for our schools and, indeed, for society as a whole. Firstly, there is the difficult issue of whether democratic ideas and values can be effectively developed in the fundamentally undemocratic, indeed authoritarian, structure of many high schools (Arnstine, 1995; Puolimatka 1995; Levin, 1998), where many teachers, never mind pupils, feel that they have little real say in the running of the school.

For schools, democratic schooling would mean there should be proper forums for discussion, consultation and decision-making involving pupils, and Article 12 of the United Nations Convention on the Rights of the Child states that young people should be consulted on issues that affect them. However, the experience of school pupil councils is not yet particularly hopeful and is discussed below. Further, the issue of democracy in the classroom is rarely raised, never mind implemented, in the school setting. Finally, in terms of rights, the whole issue of inequalities in society and their impact on the educational attainment and aspiration of school students must be taken into account, as outlined below.

Pupil councils, democracy and citizenship

'Active citizenship' has attracted the interest of researchers particularly in relation to increased student participation and the promotion of schools as democratic institutions (Harber, 2002; Kerr and Cleaver, 2004). The Advisory Group on Citizenship (1998), LTS (2002) and HMIE (2006a) state that the advent of pupil councils will enable pupils to gain an enhanced understanding of the principles of democracy and their roles as active citizens. However, they do point out that in many schools too few pupils are involved. Kerr *et al.* (2004) in their citizenship education longitudinal case study found that only 12% of pupils had been involved in pupil councils. Additionally, Cruddas (2007) and Kennedy (2007) point out that there is little opportunity for disadvantaged and marginalised students to participate and thus many voices go unheard, are sidelined or ignored.

Several authors (Davies, 2000; Lister *et al.*, 2001; Cruddas, 2007; Kennedy, 2007; Lundy, 2007; Print, 2007) highlight that students view pupil councils as ineffective and tokenistic. Cruddas (2007: p. 482) describes them as 'a form of benevolent paternalism'. Lundy (2007) states that such tokenistic opportunities to participate can be counterproductive because student voice is often not taken seriously due to the scepticism of adult concerns about giving students more control. These authors point out that students do not value pupil councils because the school appears not to value them. Concerns raised by students are that teachers predetermine which issues pupils are allowed to influence, student voice is not communicated to those who have ultimate influence over decision-making and consequently little changes. To sum up, the key critique is that the councils give the pupils voice but not agency.

Active learning and citizenship

The argument for education for citizenship and democracy is underpinned by a learning style that can be summarised as 'active learning'. In terms of classroom approach, there is much recent evidence that, when asked, pupils prefer active learning opportunities (Save the Children, 2000; 2001; Burke and Grosvenor, 2003; Ruddock and Flutter, 2004; Maitles and Gilchrist, 2006). This is not something new. John Dewey argued some 90 years ago that 'give the pupils something to do, not something to learn; and the doing is of such a nature as to demand thinking; learning naturally results' (Dewey, 1915: p. 3). The children interviewed in the sources above claimed that they enjoyed learning most when they were learning by doing; this could be practical or creative activities, talking and learning activities, school trips, speakers and contacting pupils in other countries through the internet. The word used most often to describe good lessons was 'fun'. Similarly, in her study of Swedish 11 year olds, Alerby (2003) found that the word 'fun' was used to describe positive experiences, although one cynical pupil summed up his experience as being 'during the break we have fun'.

The issue of interdisciplinary learning has been a problem in secondary schools, which has led some schools to take pupils off timetable to develop rich tasks (Maitles, 2010). Firstly, it concentrates the learning experiences of the pupils in a way that cannot be done in the formal timetabled pattern; secondly, it suggests that the key learning experiences in education for citizenship are best developed in a cross curricular method, where a number of subjects have an input; thirdly, there is evidence of deeper learning through these kinds of experiences (Dewey, 1915; Hannam, 1999; Ritchie, 1999; Save the Children, 2000, 2001; Burke and Grosvenor, 2003; MacBeath and Moos, 2004; Ruddock and Flutter, 2004; MacIntyre and Pedder, 2005; Maitles, 2005; Maitles and Gilchrist, 2006).

Hannam (2001) attempted to examine the impact of more democratic structures and participation in schools on measurable indices in UK schools. A sample of 16 schools were identified on a set of criteria as being more than usually 'student participative', and 12 agreed to participate in the study. Headteachers, other senior managers, teachers and 237 pupils were interviewed, and senior managers and the students also completed questionnaires. The overwhelming view of headteachers and other senior managers was that student participation enhanced pupil self-esteem, motivation, willingness to engage with learning, attendance rates and attainment at GCSE. Teachers in these 12 schools echoed this and added that working with these pupils was a major source of job satisfaction. The pupils regarded motivation, ownership, independence, trust, time management and responsibility as being of particular importance. Both teachers and pupils talked of improved relationships.

So far, the evidence has been anecdotal and based on experience and feelings. Yet, when compared to 'like' schools (using standard proxy means of banding schools by the aggregate socio-economic character of their pupil populations), the overall rates of exclusion were significantly lower, attendance was higher and there were consistently better-than-expected attainment at all levels of GCSE (examinations for 15–16 year olds); indeed, the gap between these 12 schools and their 'like' schools tended to increase year on year.

The small-scale nature of the survey warns us from over-generalising and there is a need for significantly expanded international research. But the premise seems sound—schools that encourage democracy and participation 'perform' better in every index, including attainment.

Even if this overstates the case, there are clearly some advantages to this approach. So, why is it not more widespread, indeed the norm? For the individual teacher, it takes courage, skill and confidence to develop active learning and genuine participation, and we need to explore the whole area of both the initial training and continuing professional development of teachers. Further, there are the anxieties of parents, who tend to judge a school solely by its exam results and believe that a traditional rote-learning, direct-teaching strategy leads to 'good' exam outcomes. This is further exacerbated by politicians and inspectorates suggesting that active learning is chaotic and might not work. And there is also a conditioned expectation by many pupils of being directed rather than becoming independent learners.

Yet, the problem is that many teachers feel vulnerable, overburdened and disempowered. One of the teacher interviewees in Gale and Densmore (2003) commented that once a policy comes out it is discussed at senior policy committees, discussed at high school senior/middle management levels and when it gets to the class teacher, most say 'I don't want to know about the politics, just tell me what to do'; they thus get 'someone else's way of interpreting that policy into their classroom'. Gale and Densmore go on to argue that there are three factors at work explaining this crisis of professionalism. Firstly, educators' isolation from each other, so that there is, in their opinion, too much 'competitive individualism' and too little shared discussion; secondly, the closing down of serious debate, in terms of the belief that classroom teachers can influence that debate; thirdly, and a result of the first two, there is a 'reduction in meaningful work' and teachers' and teacher educators' expertise is frequently dismissed, so areas of education, working through issues and perhaps problems, are appropriated by management.

The ICCS/IEA study of some 62,000 teachers in 38 countries found that the highest percentages of teachers viewed 'promoting knowledge of citizens' rights and responsibilities' as the most important aim of education for citizenship was found in Bulgaria, Chile, the Czech Republic, the Dominican Republic, Estonia, Guatemala, Indonesia, Ireland, Italy, Malta, Mexico, Paraguay, Poland, the Republic of Korea, the Russian Federation, the Slovak Republic and Thailand. In contrast, in Cyprus, Finland, Latvia, Liechtenstein, Lithuania, Slovenia, Spain and Sweden, the highest percentages were found for 'promoting students' critical and independent thinking'. The aim most frequently chosen by most teachers in Chinese Taipei and Colombia was 'developing students' skills and competencies in conflict resolution'. Only minorities of teachers viewed 'supporting the development of effective strategies for the fight against racism and xenophobia' and 'preparing students for future political participation' as among the most important objectives of civic and citizenship education.

There are other negative voices. The UK education commentator Chris Woodhead (2002: p. 3), explaining his views on classroom organisation, commented that 'Teachers teach and pupils learn. It is as simple as that.' Whilst there is an element of obvious fact in the statement (in terms of what happens), it does not reflect the reality of the attempts to introduce education for citizenship nor what goes on in many schools, nor the idea that young people are citizens now and need to participate in learning communities.

We must keep in mind that education for citizenship is still in its infancy along with debate as to its direction and effectiveness. Even when teachers are convinced of its value, the perceived needs of the curriculum, the constant flux of reform and the lack of time available can conspire to ensure that it is not well done and the pupils get more cynical about democracy, citizenship education and the motives of educators. In the words of one of Chamberlin's (2003) interviewees, 'Education for citizenship? Only if you haven't got a life!'

Inequalities in education

And yet, we must not become starry-eyed about the impact that education for citizenship (or indeed any education initiative) could have. Glaring inequalities in education, linked to inequalities in society, have a detrimental effect on education for citizenship proposals. Indeed, without an understanding of this, it becomes hard to see how education for citizenship proposals can be effective. If the general thrust of this is correct, and educational disadvantage is intrinsically linked to socio-economic disadvantage, educational reform should be viewed in terms of impacts on such inequality. Now, this must not become an excuse for inaction; the kinds of things that schools try to do to help social inclusion, such as homework clubs, breakfast sessions, positive attendance rewards and more nutritious school meals are beneficial but they cannot fundamentally alter the imbalance caused by social deprivation. New Labour from 1997 to 2010 and the Conservative/Liberal Democrat government from 2010 have been so wedded to a neo-liberal agenda that, as in health policy, no matter what government does in educational terms it does not challenge the underlying poverty which is at the root of most of the problem.

Hearts and minds

Initial training of new teachers and the continuing professional development of existing teachers needs to concentrate on winning hearts and minds to education for citizenship. Whilst education for citizenship is now a part of the curriculum in initial teacher education programmes, there is no evidence that it plays more than just a relatively cursory part, with many students able to avoid deep discussion or thought on the subject. It needs to permeate the curriculum of initial teacher education and be developed enthusiastically by tutors, particularly as student teachers and probationers are exposed to some cynical views. Maitles and Cowan (2010), in an analysis of primary school probationers in Scotland, found that whilst there is much interesting work developing, particularly in areas relating to pupil rights, eco areas, pupil councils (and consultation) and community involvement, dependent on the role of leadership in the school, there can be a key problem in that other priorities can force out citizenship initiatives.

If student teachers are the future, there is also evidence from more experienced classroom teachers that suggests there is a need for significant Continuing Professional Development in the area. Ruddock and Flutter (2004) maintain that teachers lack confidence about handling aspects of citizenship education and, as Dunkin *et al.* (1998) show in their (admittedly tiny) study of four teachers who opted into a pilot study implementing an experimental unit of work on education for citizenship, 'particular controversial content is likely to be excluded, especially if teachers lack confidence in their own mastery of that content'. This means that there is a need for both day courses in the universities on education for citizenship and modules on this integrated into Masters programmes.

Conclusion

There are further issues as yet unresolved. Firstly, is the knowledge/skills/values base adequate? Secondly, there is the issue of curriculum overload. As initiatives are piled on schools, there is the possibility of areas like education for citizenship going onto the 'back burner'. Thirdly, are teachers confident of dealing with controversial issues in the classroom?

The implementation and impact of education for citizenship initiatives depends on whether one sees the glass as half full or half empty. This book has suggested that there is excellent work going on to develop young people's interest, knowledge, skills and dispositions in areas of citizenship and democracy; yet it is very limited, indeed rare, to find examples of genuine democracy based on children's human rights. It is a matter of hearts and minds. No amount of hectoring and/or government instructions can counter this; as Bernard Crick, the person who has most lobbied for education for citizenship in UK schools, put it: 'teachers need to have a sense of mission ... to grasp the fullness of its moral and social aims' (Crick, 2000a: p. 2).

There is much to be positive about. We need to do more research into the effectiveness of citizenship in the development of positive values. However, it is also clear that we have to keep some kind of realistic perspective on the influence of education for citizenship, or any other kind of civic or political education. Education for citizenship throws up the central questions as to what sort of education we want. However, whilst there are clear benefits from education for citizenship programmes, we must be clear that no programme of education can either guarantee democratic participation or an acceptance of societal norms. Other factors, particularly socio-economic ones, impact strongly, particularly where it is perceived that governments have let down the aspirations of the population.

References

Advisory Group on Citizenship (1998) *Education for Citizenship and the Teaching of Democracy in School*, London: Qualification and Curriculum Authority

Aldrich, R. (ed.) (2002) *A Century of Education*, London: Routledge

Alerby, E. (2003) '"During the break we have fun" : a study concerning pupils' experience of school', Educational Research, Vol. 45, No. 1, pp. 17–28

Alexander, R. J. (ed.) (2009) *Children, Their World, Their Education: Final Report and Recommendations of the Cambridge Primary Review*, London: Routledge

Anderson, R. (1985) 'In search of the "lad of parts": the mythical history of Scottish education', History Workshop Journal, Vol. 19, No. 1, pp. 82–104

Appiah, K. A. (2006) *Cosmopolitanism: Ethnics in a World of Strangers*, New York: Norton

Apple, M. (2004) *Ideology and Curriculum*, London: Routledge

Apple, M. and Beane, J. (2007) *Democratic Education: Lessons in Powerful Education*, 2nd edn, Portsmouth, NH: Heinemann Press

Arnstine, D. (1995) *Democracy and the Arts of Schooling*, Albany, NY: State University of New York Press

Assessment Reform Group (2009) *Assessment in Schools: Fit for Purpose* (online). Available from: *www.tlrp.org/pub/documents/assessment.pdf* (accessed 15 June 2011)

Association of Teachers and Lecturers (ATL) (2010) 'New accountability for schools' (online). Available from: www.atl.org.uk/policy-and-campaigns/policies/new-accountability-for-schools.asp (accessed 30 April 2011)

Auden, W. H. (1934 / 1984) 'Honour: Gresham's School, Holt', in Greene, G. (ed.) (1984) *The Old School*, Oxford: Oxford University Press, pp. 1–12

Audigier, F. (2000) *Basic Concepts and Core Competencies for Education for Democratic Citizenship*, Strasbourg: Council for Europe.

Avery, P. G. and Simmons, A. M. (2008) 'Results from a three-year evaluation of teachers and students participating in the "Deliberating in a Democracy project"', paper presented at the annual meeting of the American Educational Research Association, New York, 25 March

Bailey, R. (2010) 'What's wrong with indoctrination?' (online). Available from: www.richardbailey.net/INDOCTRINATION.pdf (accessed 2 July 2011)

Banks, J. A. (2008) 'Diversity group identity, and citizenship education in a global age', Educational Researcher, Vol. 37, No. 3, pp. 129–39

Banks, J. A., Banks, C. A. M. and Clegg, A. (1999) *Teaching Strategies for the Social Studies: Decision-Making and Citizen Action*, 5th edn, New York: Longman

Barker, B. (1986) *Rescuing the Comprehensive Experience*, Milton Keynes: Open University Press

Baughman, J. E. (1975) 'An investigation of the impact of civics on political attitudes of adolescents', PhD Dissertation: University of Maryland

Baumann, Z. (1999) *In Search of Politics*, Stanford: Stanford University Press

Beane, J. A. and Apple, M. W. (1999) 'The case for democratic schools', in Apple, M. W. and Beane, J. A. (eds) (1999), *Democratic Schools, Lessons from the Chalk Face*, Buckingham: Open University Press, pp. 1–29

Bell, J. (2005) *Doing Your Research Project*, 4th edn, Maidenhead: Open University Press

Benhabib, S. (2004) *The Rights of Others: Aliens, Residents, and Citizens*, Cambridge: Cambridge University Press

Bentley, M. (1977) *The Liberal Mind 1914–1929*, Cambridge: Cambridge University Press

Benton, T., Cleaver, E., Featherstone, G., Kerr, D., Lopes, J. and Whitby, K. (2008) *Citizenship Education Longitudinal Study (CELS): Sixth Annual Report: Young People's Civic Participation In and Beyond School: Attitudes, Intentions and Influences*, Research Report DCSF-RR052, Nottingham: DCSF Publications

Bhabha, H. (1994) *The Location of Culture*, London: Routledge

Bickmore, K. (1991) 'Practicing conflict: citizenship education in high school social studies', PhD Dissertation: Stanford University

Biesta, G. (2008) 'What kind of citizen? What kind of democracy? Citizenship education and the Scottish Curriculum for Excellence', *Scottish Educational Review*, Vol. 40, No. 2, pp. 38–52

Blankenship, G. (1990) 'Classroom climate, global knowledge, global attitudes, political attitudes', *Theory and Research in Social Education*, Vol. 18, No. 4, pp. 363–86

Board of Education (1938) *Secondary Education* (Spens Report), London: HMSO

Borhaug, K. (2008) 'Educating voters: political education in Norwegian upper-secondary schools', *Journal of Curriculum Studies*, Vol. 40, No. 5, pp. 579–600

Boston J., Martin J., Pallot, J. and Walsh, P. (1996) *Public Management: The New Zealand Model*, Auckland: Oxford University Press

Bowie, J. (1975) *Penny Buff: A Clydeside School in the Thirties*, London: Constable

Bruner, J. (1966) 'Man: a course of study', in *Towards a Theory of Instruction*, Cambridge, MA: Harvard University Press, pp. 21–8

Breslin, T. (2000) 'The emerging 14–19 curriculum and qualification structure as a context for the development of citizenship education and the role of social sciences', in Lawton, D., Cairns, J. and Gardner, G. (eds) (2000) *Education for Citizenship*, London: Continuum, pp. 64–76

Bryk, A. and Schneider, B. (2002) *Trust in Schools*, New York: Russell Sage

Buie, E. (2010) 'Teacher MOT looks likely', *Times Educational Supplement*, 26 February (online). Available from: www.tes.co.uk/article.aspx?storycode=6037086 (accessed 16 June 2011)

Bullock, A. (1975) *A Language for Life, Report of the Committee of Enquiry appointed by the Secretary of State for Education and Science under the Chairmanship of Sir Alan Bullock FBA* (Bullock Report), London: HMSO

Burgess, T. (ed.) (1980) *Education for Capability*, London: NFER-Nelson

Burke, C. and Grosvenor, I. (2003) *The School I'd Like: Children and Young People's Reflections on an Education for the 21ˢᵗ Century*, London: RoutledgeFalmer

Campaign for Real Education (2006) 'Personal, Social and Health Education/Citizenship (PSHE/C): An Update' (online). Available from: www.cre.org.uk/docs/pshec-update.html (accessed 4 July 2011)

Carr, W. and Hartnett, A. (1996) *Education and the Struggle for Democracy: The Politics of Educational Ideas*, Buckingham: Open University Press

Castles, S. and Davidson, A. (2000) *Citizenship and Migration: Globalization and the Politics of Belonging*, New York: Routledge

Cecil, Lord (1940) Letter to Lord de la Warr, 21 March, *Board of Education papers*, National Archives, ED.136/129

Chamberlin, R. (2003) 'Citizenship? Only if you haven't got a life: secondary school pupils' views of citizenship education', *Westminster Studies in Education*, Vol. 26, No. 2, pp. 87–98

Chikoko, V., Gilmour J., Harber, C. and Serf, J. (2011) 'Teaching controversial issues and teacher education in England and South Africa', *Journal of Education for Teaching*, Vol. 37, No. 1, pp. 5–19

Claire, H. and Holden, C. (2007) *The Challenge of Teaching Controversial Issues*, Stoke-on-Trent: Trentham Books

Cline, W. C. (1953) 'Teaching controversial issues', *Peabody Journal of Education*, Vol. 30, No. 6, pp. 336–8

Coates, S. (2011) *First report of the Independent Review of Teachers' Standards*, London: Department for Education (online). Available from: www.education.gov.uk/publications/standard/publicationDetail/Page1/DFE-00065–2011 (accessed 16 August 2011)

Cohen, B. (1969) 'Bias and indoctrination', in Heater, D. (ed.) (1969) *The Teaching of Politics*, London: Methuen Cited in Bailey, R. (no date) 'What's Wrong With Indoctrination?' (online). Available from: www.richardbailey.net/INDOCTRINATION.pdf (accessed 9 February 2012)

Congress on Education for Democracy (1939) *Education for Democracy*, New York: Teachers College, Columbia University

Corr, H. (1990) 'An exploration into Scottish education', in Fraser, W. H. and Morris, R. J. (eds) (1990) *People and Society in Scotland, Vol II, 1830–1914*. Edinburgh: John Donald, pp. 290–309

Cotton, D. R. E. (2006) 'Teaching controversial environmental issues: neutrality and balance in the reality of the classroom', *Educational Research*, Vol. 48, No. 2, pp. 223–41

Cowan, P. and Maitles, H. (2010) 'Citizenship in primary schools: how well is it developed?', paper presented to Scottish Educational Research Association (SERA) Conference, Perth, November

Cowie, M. and Croxford, L. (2007) *Intelligent Accountability: Sound-Bite or Sea Change?* (online). Available from: *www.ces.ed.ac.uk/PDF%20Files/Brief043.pdf* (accessed 16 June 2011)

Craddock, A. (2005) 'Education for democracy in Ukraine: student learning through a US–Ukraine civic education partnership', paper presented at the College and University Faculty Assembly meeting of the National Council for the Social Studies, Kansas City, 16–18 November

Crerar, L. (2007) *Report of the Independent Review of Regulation, Audit, Inspection and Complaints Handling of Public Services in Scotland* (Crerar Report) (online). Available from: www.scotland.gov.uk/Publications/2007/09/25120506/0 (accessed 16 June 2011)

Crick, B. (2000a) 'A subject at last', *Tomorrow's Citizen*, Summer, p. 2

Crick, B. (2000b) *Essays on Citizenship*, London: Continuum

Crick, B. (2002) *Democracy: A Very Short Introduction*, Oxford: Oxford University Press

Crick, B. (2008) 'Democracy', in Arthur, J., Hahn, C. L. and Davies, I. (eds) (2008) *The Sage Handbook of Education for Citizenship and Democracy*, London: Sage, pp. 13–19

Crick, B. and Heater, D. (1977) *Essays on Political Education*, Ringmer: Falmer Press

Crick, B. and Porter, A. (1978) *Political Education and Political Literacy*, Harlow: Longmans

Croall, J. (1983) *Neill of Summerhill: The Permanent Rebel*, London: Routledge and Kegan Paul

Cruddas, L. (2007) 'Engaged voices – dialogic interaction and the construction of shared social meanings', *Educational Action Research*, Vol. 15, No. 3, pp. 479–88

Dahl, R. A. (1998) *On Democracy*, New Haven: Yale University Press

Das Gupta, M. (1997) ' "What is Indian about you?" A gendered transnational approach to ethnicity', *Gender and Society*, Vol.11, No. 5, pp. 572–96

Davies, I. (ed.) (2000) *Teaching the Holocaust*, London: Continuum

Davies, L. (2008) 'Global citizenship education', in Bajaj, M. (ed.), *Encyclopedia of Peace Education* (online). Available from: www.tc.edu/centres/epe/ (accessed 9 February 2011)

Dean, M. (1999) *Governmentality: Power and Rule in Modern Society*, London: Sage

Dearden, R. F. (1981) 'Controversial issues in the curriculum', *Journal of Curriculum Studies*, Vol. 13, No. 1 pp. 37–44

Department for Education (2011) *National Curriculum Review Launched*, press notice, 20 January (online). Available from: www.education.gov.uk/inthenews/pressnotices/a0073149/national-curriculum-review-launched (accessed 25 February 2011)

De Tocqueville, A. and Commager, H. S. (1835–40 / 1946) *Democracy in America*, Oxford: Oxford University Press

Deuchar, R. (2004) 'Reconciling self interest and ethics: the role of primary school pupil councils', *Scottish Educational Review*, Vol. 36, No. 2, pp. 159–68

Deuchar, R. (2009) 'Seen and heard, and then not heard: Scottish pupils' experience of democratic educational practice during the transition from primary to secondary school', *Oxford Review of Education*, Vol. 35, No. 1, pp. 23–40

Devine, T. M. (2000) *The Scottish Nation 1700–2000*, London: Penguin

Dewey, J. (1899 / 1967) *The School and Society*, revised edn, Chicago: University of Chicago Press

Dewey, J. (1915) *The School and Society*, Chicago: University of Chicago Press

Dewey, J. (1916 / 1944) *Democracy and Education*, New York: Free Press

Dewey, J. (1937) 'Democracy and educational administration', in Ratner, J. (ed.) (1939) *Intelligence in the Modern World: John Dewey's Philosophy,* New York: Modern Library, pp. 400–1

Donaldson, G. H. C. (2011) *Teaching Scotland's Future – Report of a Review of Teacher Education in Scotland* (Donaldson Report) (online). Available from: www.scotland.gov.uk/Publications/2011/01/13092132/15 (accessed 16 June 2011)

Duncan, A. (2011) 'The social studies are essential to a well-rounded education', *Social Education*, Vol. 75, No. 3 pp. 124–5

Dunkin, M., Welch, A., Merritt, R., Phillips, R. and Craven, R. (1998) '"Teachers" explanations of classroom events: knowledge and beliefs about teaching civics and citizenship', *Teaching and Teacher Education*, Vol. 14, No. 2, pp. 141–51

Dweck, C. (2007) *Mindset: The New Psychology of Success*, New York: Ballantine Books,

Eccles, J. R. (1948) *My Life as a Public School Master*, Blackburn: 'The Times' Printing Works

Ehman, L. (1969) 'An analysis of the relationships of selected educational variables with the political socialization of high school students', *American Educational Research Journal*, Vol. 6, No. 4, pp. 559–80

Ehman, L. (1970) 'Normative discourse and attitude changes in the social studies classroom', *The High School Journal*, Vol. 54, No. 1, pp. 76–83

Engle, S. and Ochoa, A. (1988) *Education for Democratic Citizenship: Decision-Making in the Social Studies*, New York: Teachers' College Press

Etzioni, A. (1997) *The New Golden Rule: Community and Morality in a Democratic Society*, London: Profile Books

Evans, R. W. and Saxe, D. W. (eds) (1996) *Handbook on Teaching Social Issues*, Washington, DC: National Council for the Social Studies

Fielding, M. and Bragg, S. (2003) *Students as Researchers: Making a Difference*, Cambridge: Pearson

Fielding, M. (2009) 'Public space and educational leadership: Reclaiming and renewing our radical traditions', *Educational Management, Administration and Leadership*, Vol. 37, No. 4, pp. 497–521

Finer, S. E. (1970) *Comparative Government*, London: Penguin

Franklin, B. M. and McCulloch, G. (2003) 'Partnerships in a "cold climate": the case of Britain', in Franklin, B. M., Bloch, M. N. and Popkewitz, T. S. (eds) (2003) *Educational Partnerships and the State: The Paradoxes of Governing Schools, Children and Families*, New York: Palgrave Macmillan, pp. 83–107

Franklin, B. M., Bloch, M. N. and Popkewitz, T. S. (eds) (2003) *Educational Partnerships and the State: The Paradoxes of Governing Schools, Children and Families*, New York: Palgrave Macmillan

Freire, P. (1998) *Pedagogy of Freedom: Ethics, Democracy, and Civic Courage*, Lanham: Rowman & Littlefield

Foucault, M. (1991) 'Governmentalité', in Burcell, G., Gordon, C. and Miller, P. (eds) (1991) *The Foucault Effect: Studies in Governmentality*, Hemel Hempstead: Harvester Wheatsheaf, pp. 87–104

Fullan, M. (2003) *The Moral Imperative of School Leadership*, Thousand Oaks, CA: Corwin Press

Furedi, F. (2009) 'Turning children into Orwellian eco-spies', *Spiked* (online.) Available from: www.spiked-online.com/index.php/site/article/7830/ (accessed 4 July 2011)

Furman, G. C. and Starrat, R. J. (2002) 'Leadership for democratic community in schools', in Murphy, J. (ed.) (2002) *The Educational Leadership Challenge*, Chicago: University of Chicago Press, pp. 105–33

Gale, T. and Densmore, K. (2003) *Engaging Teachers*, Maidenhead: Open University Press

Gaventa, J. (2002) 'Exploring citizenship, participation and accountability', *IDS Bulletin*, Vol. 33, No. 2, pp. 1–11

General Teaching Council of Scotland (2006a) *The Standard for Full Registration* (online). Available from: www.gtcs.org.uk/standards/standard-full-registration.aspx (accessed 4 July 2011)

General Teaching Council of Scotland (2006b) *Standard for Initial Teacher Education (SITE)* (online). Available from: www.gtcs.org.uk/standards/standard-initial-teacher-education.aspx (accessed 15 July 2011)

Gibson W. J. (1912) *Education in Scotland: A Sketch of the Past and the Present*, London: Longmans, Green

Gillborn, D. (2006) 'Citizenship education as placebo: 'standards', institutional racism and education policy', *Education, Citizenship and Social Justice*, Vol. 1, No. 1, pp. 83–104

Gillborn, D. and Youdell, D. (2000) *Rationing Education*, London: Open University Press

Goddard, T. (2004) 'The role of school leaders in establishing democratic principles in a post-conflict society', *Journal of Educational Administration*, Vol. 42, No. 6, pp. 685–96

Grant, S. G., and Salinas, C. (2008) 'Assessment and accountability in the social studies', in

C. Tyson, & L. Levstick (Eds.), *Handbook of Research on Social Studies Education*, New York: Routledge pp. 219–36

Green, F. T. (1972) 'Indoctrination and beliefs', in Snook, I. A. (ed.) (1972) *Concepts of Indoctrination: Philosophical Essays*, London: Routledge and Kegan Paul, pp. 25–46

Griffin, A. F. (1942 / 1992) *A Philosophical Approach to the Subject Matter Preparation of Teachers of History*, Washington, DC: National Council of the Social Studies. Reprinted from a doctoral dissertation, Ohio State University, 1942

Gutmann, A. (1987) *Democratic Education*, Princeton: Princeton University Press

Habermas, J. (1984) *The Theory of Communicative Action – Reason and the Rationalization of Society* (1), Boston: Beacon Press

Habermas, J. (2001) Warum Braucht Europa Eine Verfassung? *Die Zeit*, 28 June (online). Available from: www.zeit.de/2001/27/200127_verfassung.xml (accessed 1 June 2011)

Hahn, C. L. (1984) 'The freedom to teach and to learn is basic', *Georgia Council for the Social Sciences*, Vol. 15, No. 2, pp. 1–7

Hahn, C. L. (1996a) 'Research on issues-centered social studies', in Evans, R. and Saxe, D. W. (eds) (1996) *Handbook on Issues-centered Teaching and Learning*, Washington, DC: National Council for the Social Studies, pp. 25–44

Hahn, C. L. (1996b) 'Gender and political learning', *Theory and Research in Social Education*, Vol. 24, No. 1, pp. 8–35

Hahn, C. L. (1998) *Becoming Political: Comparative Perspectives on Citizenship Education*, Albany, NY: State University of New York Press

Hahn, C. L. (1999) 'Challenges to civic education in the United States', in Torney-Purta, J., Schwille, J. and Amadeo, J. (eds) (1998) *Civic Education Across Countries: Twenty-Four National Case Studies from the IEA Civic Education Project*, Amsterdam: International Association for the Evaluation of Educational Achievement, pp. 583–607

Hahn, C. L. (2010) 'Issues-centred pedagogy and classroom climate for discussion: a view from the United States', in Kennedy, K., Lee, W. O. and Grossman, D. (eds) (2010) *Citizenship Education Pedagogies in Asia and the Pacific*, Hong Kong: Springer, pp. 315–31

Halpern, D. (2010) *The Hidden Wealth of Nations*, Cambridge: Polity Press

Halsey, A. H. (1978) *The Reith Lectures: Change in British Society*, Lecture 1: To Know Ourselves (online), Available from: www.bbc.co.uk/programmes/p00h4qmd (accessed 16 June 2011)

Hammond, J. and Looney, A. (2000) 'Revisioning citizenship education: the Irish experience', in Lawton, D., Cairns, J. and Gardner, R. (eds) (2000) *Education for Citizenship*, London: Continuum, pp. 175–82

Hannam, D. (1999) 'Learning democracy is more than just learning about democracy', paper presented at GLO [Danish Union of Upper Secondary Students] conference, Denmark, October

Hannam, D. (2001) *A Pilot Study to Evaluate the Impact of the Student Participation Aspects of the Citizenship Order on Standards of Education in Secondary Schools, A Report to the DfEE*, London: CSV

Harber, C. (2002) 'Not quite the revolution: citizenship education in England', in Schweisfurth, M., Davies, L. and Harber, C. (eds) (2002) *Learning Democracy and Citizenship*, Oxford: Symposium Books, pp. 225–39

Harrison, J. F. C. (1961) *Learning and Living, 1790–1960: A Study in the History of the English Adult Education Movement*, London: Routledge and Kegan Paul

Hart, S., Dixon, A., Drummond, M. and McIntyre, D. (2004) *Learning Without Limits*, Maidenhead: Open University Press

Hess, D. E. (2002) 'Discussing controversial public issues in secondary social studies classrooms: learning from skilled teachers', *Theory and Research in Social Education*, Vol. 30, No. 1, pp. 10–41

Hess, D. (2009) *Controversy in the Classroom: The Democratic Power of Discussion*, New York: Routledge

Hess, D. (2010) Personal communication, 1 March

Hess, D. and Avery, P. (2008) 'Discussion of controversial issues as a form and goal of democratic education', in Arthur, J., Davies, I. and Hahn, C. (eds) (2008) *The Sage Handbook of Education for Citizenship and Democracy*, London: Sage, pp. 506–18

HMIE [Her Majesty's Inspectorate of Education] (2002) *How Good Is Our School?, Self-evaluation Series E: Education for Citizenship* (online). Available from: *www.hmie.gov.uk/documents/publication/hgiospwp.pdf* (accessed 30 June 2011)

HMIE (2003) *Taking a Closer look at Citizenship* (online). Available from: *www.hmie.gov.uk/documents/publication/efcpcp1.pdf* (accessed 30 June 2011)

HMIE (2006a) *Education for Citizenship, A Portrait of Current Practice in Scottish Schools and Pre-school Centres*, Livingston: HMIe (online). Available from: www.hmie.gov.uk/documents/publication/efcpcp1.pdf (accessed 16 June 2011)

HMIE (2006b) *Improving Scottish Education 2003–2005* (online). Available from: *www.hmie.gov.uk/documents/publication/hmieise.pdf (accessed 30 June 2011)*

HMIE (2006c) *Report to SEED on the Delivery of the National Priorities* (online). Available from: www.hmie.gov.uk/documents/publication/hmiednp-02.html (accessed 16 June 2011)

HMIE (2007a) *How Good Is Our School? How Good Can We Be?* (online). Available from: www.hmie.gov.uk/documents/publication/hgiosjte3.pdf (accessed 15 June 2011)

HMIE (2007b) *Journey to Excellence* (online). Available from: www.journeytoexcellence.org.uk/ (accessed 16 June 2011)

HMIE (2009) *Improving Scottish Education, A Report on Inspection and Review 2005–2008* (online). Available from: www.hmie.gov.uk/documents/publication/ise09pdf (accessed 16 June 2011)

HMIE (online) Reports on individual Scottish schools. Available from: www.hmie.gov.uk/SelectEstablishment.aspx?typeid=3 (accessed 15 June 2011)

HMSO (2000) *Standards in Scotland's Schools etc. Act*, Edinburgh: HMSO

Holden, C. and Minty, S. (2011) 'Going global: Young Europeans' aspirations and actions for the future', *Citizenship, Teaching and Learning*, Vol. 6, No. 2, pp. 123–38

Hubback, E. and Simon, E. (1934) *Education for Citizenship*, London: AEC

Humes, W. M. (1986) *The Leadership Class in Scottish Education*, Edinburgh: John Donald

Humes, W. M. and Bryce, T. G. K. (2008) 'The distinctiveness of Scottish education', in Bryce, T. G. K. and Humes, W. M. (eds) (2008) *Scottish Education*, 3rd edn, Edinburgh: Edinburgh University Press, pp. 98-112

Hunt, M. P. and Metcalf, L. E. (1955 / 1968) *Teaching High School Social Studies: Problems in Reflective Thinking and Social Understanding*, New York: Harper and Bros

Jackson, P. W. (1968) *Life in Classrooms*, New York: Teachers College Press

James, A. (2010) 'To be (come) or not to be (come): understanding children's citizenship', *ANNALS of the American Academy of Political and Social Science*, Vol. 633, No. 1, pp. 167–79

JanMohamed, A. (1987) 'Toward a theory of minority discourse', *Cultural Critique 6*, Spring, pp. 5–11

Jansen, T., Chioncel, N. and Dekker, K. (2006) 'Social cohesion and integration: Learning active citizenship', *British Journal of Sociology of Education*, Vol. 27, No. 2, pp. 189–205

Johnson, N. B. (1980) 'The material culture of public school classrooms: the symbolic integration of local schools and national culture', *Anthropology & Education Quarterly*, Vol. 11, No. 3, pp. 173–90

Kahne, J. and Sporte, S. (2008) 'Developing citizens: the impact of civic learning opportunities on students' commitment to civic participation', *American Educational Research Journal*, Vol. 20, No. 10, pp. 1–29

Kennedy, K. (2007) 'Student constructions of "active citizenship": what does participation mean to students?', *British Journal of Educational Studies*, Vol. 55, No. 3, pp. 304–24

Kerr, D. and Cleaver, E. (2004) *Citizenship Education Longitudinal Study: Literature Review – Citizenship Education One Year On – What Does It Mean?: Emerging Definitions and Approaches in the First Year of National Curriculum Citizenship in England*, DfES Research Report 532, Nottingham: DfES

Kerr, D., Ireland, E., Lopes, J., Craig, R. and Cleaver, E. (2004) *Citizenship Education Longitudinal Study: Second Annual Report: First Longitudinal Survey Making Citizenship Education Real*, DfES Research Report 531, Nottingham: DfES

Kiwan, D. (2008) *Education for Inclusive Citizenship*, Abingdon: Routledge

Kohlberg, L. (1982) 'Recent work in moral education', in Ward, L. A. (ed.) (1982) *The Ethical Dimension of the School Curriculum*, Swansea: Pineridge Press, pp. 23–35

Ladson-Billings, G. (2004) 'Culture versus citizenship: the challenge of racialized citizenship in the United States', in Banks, J. A. (ed.) (2004) *Diversity and Citizenship Education*, San Francisco: Jossey-Bass/Wiley, pp. 99–126

Laursen, P. F. (2007) 'Tugt, Disciplin Og Ledelse [Chastigate, Disciplin, Leadership]', in Moos, L., Brad, K. B., Kofod, K. K., Laursen, P. F., Holm, L., Krejsler, J., Kryger, N., Ravn, B., Knudsen, H., Bovbjerg, K. M. and Sorensen, M. S. (eds) (2007) *Nye Sociale Teknologier I Folkeskolen*, Frederikshavn: Dafolo, pp. 53–66

Law, S. (2006) *The War for Children's Minds*, London: Routledge

Lawson, H. (2001) 'Active citizenship in schools and the community', *Curriculum Journal*, Vol. 12, No. 2, pp. 163–78

Learning and Teaching Scotland (1996) *Teaching for Effective Learning* (online). Available from: www.ltscotland.org.uk/curriculumforexcellence/buildingthecurriculum/guidance (accessed 16 June 2011)

Learning and Teaching Scotland (2002) *Education for Citizenship – A Paper for Discussion and Development*, Dundee: Learning and Teaching Scotland

Learning and Teaching Scotland (2006–10) *Building the Curriculum 1–5 series* (online). Available from: www.ltscotland.org.uk/curriculumforexcellence/buildingthecurriculum/guidance/ (accessed 16 June 2011)

Learning and Teaching Scotland (2009) *Curriculum for Excellence: Experiences and Outcomes* (online). Available from: www.ltscotland.org.uk/curriculumforexcellence/experiencesandoutcomes/index.asp (accessed 16 June 2011)

Learning and Teaching Scotland (2011) *What is Curriculum for Excellence* (online). Available from: www.ltscotland.org.uk/understandingthecurriculum/whatiscurriculumforexcellence/index.asp (accessed 15 June 2011)

Lee, H. D. P. (1955) *Plato: The Republic*, Harmondsworth: Penguin

Leighton, R. (2006) 'Revisiting Postman and Weingartner's 'New Education' – is teaching citizenship a subversive activity?', *Citizenship and Teacher Education*, Vol. 2, No. 1, pp. 79–89

Leitch, R., Gardner, J., Mitchell, S., Lundy, L., Clough, P., Galanouli, D. and Odena,

S. (2006) 'Researching creatively with pupils in Assessment for Learning (AfL) classrooms on experiences of participation and consultation', Paper presented at the European Education Research Association Annual Conference, Switzerland

Leitch Review of Skills (2006) *Prosperity for All in the Global Economy: World Class Skills*, London: H.M. Treasury

Levin, B. (1998) 'The educational requirement for democracy', *Curriculum Inquiry*, Vol. 28, No. 1, pp. 57–79

Levinson, R. (2006) 'Towards a theoretical framework for teaching controversial socio-scientific issues', *International Journal of Science Education*, Vol. 28, No. 10, pp. 1201–24

Limage, L. J. (2001) 'Introduction: alternative perspectives on democracy and education', in Limage, L. (ed.) (2001) *Democratising Education and Educating Democratic Citizens: International and Historical Perspectives*, London: RoutledgeFalmer, pp. xiii–xxii

Lister, R., Middleton, S. and Smith, N. (2001) *Young People's Voices*, Leicester: National Youth Agency

Lister, R. (2008) 'Inclusive citizenship, gender and poverty: some implications for education for citizenship', *Citizenship, Teaching and Learning*, Vol. 4, No. 1, pp. 3–19

Loewen, J. (2010) *Teaching What Really Happened: How to Avoid the Tyranny of Textbooks and Get Students Excited About Doing History*, New York: Teachers College Press

Louis, K. S. (2003) 'Democratic schools, democratic communities', *Leadership and Policy in Schools*, Vol. 2, No. 2, pp. 93–108

Lugg, C. A., Bulkey, K., Firestone, W. A. and Garner, C. W. (2002) 'The contextual terrain facing educational leaders' in Murphy, J. (ed.) (2002) *The Educational Leadership Challenge: Redefining Leadership for the 21th Century*, Chicago: University of Chicago Press, pp. 20–41

Lundahl, L. (2002) 'Education and the democratic society', *European Educational Research Journal*, Vol. 1, No. 4, pp. 742–50

Lundy, L. (2007) '"Voice" is not enough: conceptualising Article 12 of the United Nations convention on the rights of the child', *British Educational Research Journal*, Vol. 33, No. 6, pp. 927–42

MacBeath, J. and Moos, L. (eds) (2004) *Democratic Learning: the Challenge to School Effectiveness*, London: RoutledgeFalmer

MacIntyre, D. and Pedder, D. (2005) 'The impact of pupil consultation on classroom practice', in Arnott, M., MacIntyre, D., Pedder, D. and Reay, D. (eds) (2005) *Consultation in the Classroom*, Cambridge: Pearson, pp. 7–41

Maddern, K. (2009) 'Pupil voice dubbed failure by children's commissioner' , *Times Educational Supplement*, 27 November

Maira, S. (2005) 'The intimate and the imperial: South Asian Muslim immigrant youth after 9/11', in Maira, S. and Soep, E. (eds) (2005) *Youthscapes: The Popular, the National, the Global*, Philadelphia: University of Pennsylvania Press, pp. 64–84

Maitles, H. (2000) 'Thirty years of teaching political literacy in Scottish schools: how effective is modern studies?' in Lawton, D., Cairns, J. and Gardner, R. (eds) (2000) *Education for Citizenship*, London: Continuum, pp. 162–74

Maitles, H. (2005) *Values in Education: We're All Citizens Now*, Edinburgh: Dunedin Academic Press

Maitles, H. (2010) 'Citizenship initiatives and pupil values: a case study of one Scottish school's experience', *Educational Review*, Vol. 62, No.4, pp. 391–406

Maitles, H. and Deuchar, R. (2004) '"Why are they bombing innocent Iraqis?": political literacy among primary pupils', *Improving Schools*, Vol. 7, No. 1, pp. 97–105

Maitles, H. and Gilchrist, I. (2005) 'We're citizens now!: The development of positive values through a democratic approach to learning', *Journal for Critical Education Policy*, Vol. 3, No. 1 (online). Available from: www.jceps.com/?pageID=article&articleID=45 (accessed 16 June 2011)

Maitles, H. and Gilchrist, I. (2006) 'Never too young to learn democracy!: A case study of a democratic approach to learning in a religious and moral education secondary class in the West of Scotland', *Educational Review*, Vol. 58, No. 1, pp. 67–85

Makrinioti, D. and Solomon, J. (1999) 'The discourse of citizenship education in Greece: national identity and social diversity', in Torney-Purta, J., Schwille, J. and Amadeo, J. (eds) (1999) *Civic Education Across Countries – Twenty Four National Case Studies from the IEA Civic Educational Project*, Amsterdam: International Association for the Evaluation of Educational Achievement, pp. 285–312

Marshall, T. H. (1950) *Citizenship and Social Class and Other Essays*, Cambridge: Cambridge University Press

Mau, S., Mewes, J. and Zimmermann, A. (2008) 'Cosmopolitan attitudes through transnational social practices?', *Global Networks*, Vol. 8, No. 1, pp. 1–24

McCarthy, C. (1998) *The Uses of Culture Education and the Limits of Ethnic Affiliation*, New York and London: Routledge

McCowan, T. (2009) *Rethinking Citizenship Education*, London and New York, Continuum

McCulloch, G. (1994) *Educational Reconstruction: The 1944 Education Act and the Twenty-First Century*, London: Woburn

McCulloch, G. (2001) 'The reinvention of teacher professionalism', in Phillips, R. and Furlong, J. (ed.) (2001) *Education, Reform and the State: Twenty-Five Years of Politics, Policy and Practice*, London: RoutledgeFalmer, pp. 103–17

McCulloch, G. (2004) 'From incorporation to privatization: public and private secondary education in twentieth-century England', in Aldrich, R. (ed.) (2004) *Public or Private Education? Lessons from History*, London: Woburn, pp. 53–72

McCulloch, G. (2007) *Cyril Norwood and the Ideal of Secondary Education*, New York: Palgrave Macmillan

McCulloch, G. (2011) 'Education policy and practice', in Wadsworth, M. and Bynner, J. (eds) (2011) *A Companion to Life Course Studies: The Social and Historical Context of the British Birth Cohort Studies*, London: Routledge, pp. 69–90

McCulloch, G., Helsby, G. and Knight, P. (2000) *The Politics of Professionalism: Teachers and the Curriculum*, London: Continuum

McCulloch, G. and Woodin, T. (2010) 'Learning and liberal education: the case of the Simon Family, 1912–1939', *Oxford Review of Education*, Vol. 36, No. 2, pp. 187–201

McLaughlin, T. (2003) 'Teaching controversial issues in citizenship education', in Lockyer, A., Crick, B. and Annnette, J. (eds) (2003) *Education for Democratic Citizenship: Issues of Theory and Practice*, Aldershot: Ashgate, pp. 149–60

McLean, A. (2009) *Motivating Every Learner*, London: Sage

McPherson, A, A. and Raab, C. D. (1988) *Governing Education: A Sociology of Policy Since 1945*, Edinburgh: Edinburgh University Press

Midwinter, E. (1975) *Education and the Community*, London: Allen and Unwin

Mills, C. W. (1959) *The Sociological Imagination*, New York: Oxford University Press

Moos, L. (2003) 'Introduction', in MacBeath, J. and Moos, L. (eds) (2003) *Democratic Learning: The Challenge to School Effectiveness*, London: RoutledgeFalmer, pp. 1–18

Moos, L. (2009) 'Hard and soft governance: the journey from transnational agencies to school leadership', *European Educational Research Journal*, Vol. 8, No. 3, pp. 397–406

Moos, L. (2010) 'From successful school leadership towards leadership in webs', in Huber, S., Saravanabhavan, R. and Hader-Popp, S. (eds) (2010) *School Leadership – International Perspectives*, Dordrecht: Springer, pp. 121–4

Moos, L. (2011) 'Sustaining leadership through self-renewing communication', in Moos *et al.* (eds) (2011), pp. 127–49

Moos, L., Johansson, O. and Day, C. (eds) (2011) *How School Principals Sustain Success over Time*, Dordrecht: Springer

Moos, L. and Kofod, K. K. (2011) 'Danish successful school leadership – revisited', in Moos *et al.* (eds) (2011), pp. 39–54

Moos, L., Skedsmo, G., Höög, J., Olofsson, A. and Johnson, L. (2011) 'The hurricate of accountabilities? Comparisons of accountability comprehensions and practices', in Moos *et al.* (eds) (2011), pp. 199–222

Munro, N. (2010) 'Education Secretary calls for inspection shake-up', *Times Educational Supplement*, 26 February (online). Available from: www.tes.co.uk/article. aspx?storycode=6037088 (accessed 16 June 2011)

Murphy, D. (2007) *Professional School Leadership: Dealing with Dilemmas*, Edinburgh: Dunedin Academic Press

Murtagh, C. (2010) 'Checking up: Is it time for a rethink of the school inspection system?', *Holyrood Magazine*, 15 February

National Council for the Social Studies (1977) 'The treatment of controversial issues in schools', in Cox, B. (ed.) *The Censorship Game and How to Play It*, Washington, DC: National Council for the Social Studies, pp. 26–30

National Council for the Social Studies (2007) *Academic Freedom and the Social Studies Teacher: A Position Statement of the National Council for the Social Studies* (online). Available from: www.socialstudies.org/positions/academicfreedom (accessed 7 November 2008)

National Council for the Social Studies (2011) '2010 NCSS House of Delegates Resolutions', *Social Education*, Vol. 75, No. 3, p. 168

Nelson, J. L. and Hahn, C. L. (2010) 'The need for courage in American schools: cases and causes', *Social Education*, Vol. 74, No. 6, pp. 298–303

Nelson, L. (1970) *Die Unmöglichkeit der Erkenntnistheorie* (1911), Gesammelts Schriften, Vol. II, Hamburg; Felix Meiner Verlag

Newmann, F. M. and Oliver, D. W. (1970) *Clarifying Public Controversy: An Approach to Teaching Social Studies*, Boston: Little, Brown

Nichols, S. L. and Berliner, D. C. (2007) *Collateral Damage. How High-Stakes Testing Corrupts American Schools*, Cambridge, MA: Harvard Educational Press

Nieto, S. (2002) *Language, Culture, and Teaching: Critical Perspectives for a New Century*, Mahwah, NJ: Lawrence Erlbaum Associates

Norwood, C. (1940) 'The crisis in education – I', *Spectator*, 9 February, p. 176

Nussbaum, M. (2002) 'Patriotism and cosmopolitanism', in Cohen, J. (ed.) (2002) *For Love of Country*, Boston: Beacon Press, pp. 2–17

Oakeshott, M. (1989) 'A place of learning', in Fuller, T. (ed.) (1989) *Michael Oakeshott on Education*, New Haven: Yale University Press, pp.17–42

Ochoa, A. (1979) 'Censorship: does anybody care?', *Social Education*, Vol. 43, No. 4, pp. 304–9

OECD (2007) *Quality and Equity of Schooling in Scotland*, Paris: Organization for Economic Cooperation and Development

Oettingen, A. V. (2001) *Det pædagogiske paradoks* [The Pedagogical Paradox], Århus: Klim

References

Ofsted (2006 / 2009) The Wroxham School Inspection Reports (online). Available from: www.ofsted.gov.uk/inspection-reports/find-inspection-report/provider/ELS/117566 (accessed 15 June 2011)

Ofsted (2009) *The Evaluation schedule for schools. Guidance and grade descriptors for inspecting schools in England under section 5 of the Education Act 2005 from September 2009*, London: HMSO

Ofsted (2010) *Citizenship established? Citizenship in schools 2006–2009* (online). Available from: www.teachingcitizenship.org.uk/dnloads/citizenship_established.pdf (accessed 9 February 2012)

Oliver, D. W. and Shaver, J. P. (1966) *Teaching Public Issues in the High School*, Boston: Houghton-Mifflin

O'Neill, O. (2002) *The Reith Lectures: A Question of Trust, Lecture 3:* Called to Account (online). Available from: www.bbc.co.uk/radio4/reith2002/lecture3.shtml (accessed 16 June 2011)

Osler, A. and Starkey, H. (2000) 'Citizenship, human rights and cultural diversity', in Osler, A. (ed.) (2001) *Citizenship and Democracy in Schools: Diversity, Identity, Equality*, Stoke-on-Trent: Trentham Books, pp. 3–17

Osler, A. and Starkey, H. (2005) *Changing Citizenship: Democracy and Inclusion in Education*, Maidenhead: Open University Press

Ozouf, J. (1967) *Nous Les Maitres D'ecole: Autobiographies D'instituteurs de la Belle Epoque*, Paris: Julliard

Parker, W. C. (1996) *Educating the Democratic Mind*, Albany, NY: State University of New York Press

Parker, W. C. (2006) 'Public discourses in schools: purposes, problems, possibilities', *Educational Researcher*, Vol. 35, No. 8, pp. 11–18

Paterson, L. (2003) *Scottish Education in the Twentieth Century*, Edinburgh: Edinburgh University Press

Pattie, C. (2004) *Citizenship in Britain; Values, Participation and Democracy*, Cambridge: Cambridge University Press

Perlinger, A., Canetti-Nisim, D. and Pedahzur, A. (2006) 'Democratic attitudes among high school pupils: the role played by perceptions of class climates', *School Effectiveness and School Improvement*, Vol. 17, No. 1, pp. 119–40

Peters, M., Marshall, J. and Fitzsimons, P. (2000) 'Managerialism and educational policy in a global context: Foucault, neoliberalism and the doctrine of self-management', in Burbules, N. C. and Torres, C. A. (eds) (2000) *Globalization and Education: Critical Perspectives*, New York: Routledge, pp. 109–32

Philips, R. (2000) 'Culture, community and citizenship in Wales: citizenship education for the new democracy?', in Lawton, D., Cairns, J. and Gardner, R. (eds) (2000) *Education for Citizenship*, London: Continuum, pp. 151–61

Porter, A. (1979) 'The programme for political education: a guide for beginners', *Social Science Teacher*, Vol. 8, No. 3, pp. 98–106

Pring, R., Hayward, G., Hodgson, A., Johnson, J., Keep, E., Oancea, A., Rees, G., Spours, K. and Wilde, S. (2009) *Education for All: the Future of Education and Training for 14–19 Year Olds*, London: Routledge

Print, M. (2007) 'Citizenship education and youth participation in democracy', *British Journal of Educational Studies*, Vol. 55, No. 3, pp. 325–45

Puolimatka, T. (1995) *Democracy and Education: The Critical Citizen as an Educational Aim*, Helsinki: Suomalainen Tiedeakatemia

Pykett, J. (2007) 'Making citizens governable? The Crick Report as governmental technology', *Journal of Education Policy*, Vol. 22, No. 3, pp. 301–19

QCA (1998) *Education for Citizenship and the Teaching of Democracy in Schools* (Crick Report), London: Qualifications and Curriculum Authority

Ranson, S. (1990) 'From 1944 to 1988: education, citizenship and democracy', in Flude, M. and Hammer, M. (eds) (1998) *The Education Reform Act, 1988: Its Origins and Implications*, London: Falmer, pp. 1–19

Reay, D. (2008) 'Tony Blair, the promotion of the "active" educational citizen, and middle-class hegemony', *Oxford Review of Education*, Vol. 34, No. 6, pp. 639–50

Ritchie, A. (1999) *Our Lives Consultation: Final Report*, Edinburgh: Save the Children Scotland

Rizvi, F. (1993) 'Children and the grammar of popular racism', in McCarthy, C. and Crichlow, W. (eds) (1993) *Race, Identity and Representation in Education*, New York and London: Routledge, pp. 126–39

Rizvi, F. and Lingard, B. (2006) 'Globalization and the changing nature of the OECD's educational work', in Lauder, H., Brown, P., Dillabough, J. A. and Halsey, A. H. (eds) (2006) *Education, Globalization, and Social Change*, Oxford: Oxford University Press, pp. 247–60

Rizvi, F. and Lingard, B. (2010) *Globalizing Education Policy*, London: Routledge

Rooney, K. (2007) 'Citizenship education: making kids conform', *Spiked* (online). Available from: www.spiked-online.com/index.php?/site/printable/4023/ (accessed 30 April 2011)

Ruddock, J. (1983) *The Humanities Curriculum Project: An Introduction*, Norwich: University of East Anglia

Ruddock, J. and Flutter, J. (2004) *How To Improve Your School*, London: Continuum

Sacks, J. (1997) *The Politics of Hope*, London: Jonathan Cape

Sagan, C. (1996) *The Demon-Haunted World: Science as a Candle in the Dark*, New York: Ballantine Books

Save the Children (2000) *'It's Our Education': Young People's Views on Improving Their Schools*, Edinburgh: Save the Children Scotland

Save the Children (2001) *Education for Citizenship in Scotland: Perspectives of Young People*, Edinburgh: Save the Children Scotland

Schulz, W., Ainley, J., Fraillon, J., Kerr, D. and Losito, B. (2010) *International Findings from the IEA International Civic and Citizenship Education Study*, Amsterdam: International Association for the Evaluation of Educational Achievement

Scottish Executive (2004a) *Ambitious Excellent Schools: Our Agenda for Action* (online). Available from: www.scotland.gov.uk/Publications/2004/11/20176/45852 (accessed 16 June 2011)

Scottish Executive (2004b) *A Curriculum for Excellence*, Edinburgh: Scottish Executive

Searle, C. (1975) *Classrooms of Resistance*, London: Writers and Readers Publishing Co-operative

SED [Scottish Education Department] (1977a) *The Structure of the Curriculum in the Third and Fourth Years of the Scottish Secondary School* (Munn Report), Edinburgh: HMSO

SED (1977b) *Assessment for All* (Dunning Report), Edinburgh: HMSO

SEED [Scottish Executive Education Department] (2003) *National Debate on Education, news release* (online). Available from: www.scotland.gov.uk/News/Releases/2003/01/3009 (accessed 16 June 2011)

Selby-Bigge, L. (1927) *The Board of Education*, London: Putnam and Sons

SFRE [Strategic Forum for Research in Education] (2010) Unlocking Learning? Towards Evidence-Informed Policy and Practice in Education Research Briefing (online). Available from: www.sfre.ac.uk/wp-content/uploads/2010/07/Final-SFRE-Briefing1.pdf (accessed 8 August 2011)

Simon, E. (1934) Letter to Brian Simon, 21 November, *Brian Simon papers*, Institute of Education: University of London

Simon, E. (1935a) Letter to Brian Simon, 9 January, *Brian Simon papers*, Institute of Education: University of London

Simon, E. (1935b) 'The aims of education for citizenship', in Association for Education in Citizenship (ed.) (1935) *Education for Citizenship in Secondary Schools*, London: AEC, pp. 1–10

Simpson, J. H. (1925) *Howson of Holt: A Study in School Life*, London: Sidgwick and Jackson

Singleton, L. (1996) 'Preparing citizens to participate in democratic discourse: the public issues model', in Evans, R. W. and Saxe, D. W. (eds) (1996) *Handbook on Teaching Social Issues*, Washington, DC: National Council for the Social Studies, pp. 59–65

Smith, H. Bombas (1927) *The Nation's Schools: Their Task and Their Importance*, London: Longmans, Green

Smith, M. K. and Doyle, M. (2002) 'Globalization', *Encyclopedia of Informal Education* (online). Available from: www.infed.org/biblio/globalization.htm (accessed 15 June 2011)

Spencer, S. (2000) 'The implication of the human rights act for education', in Ostler, A. (ed.) (2000) *Citizenship and Democracy in Schools: Diversity, Identity, Equality*, Stoke-on-Trent: Trentham Books, pp. 19–32

Spens, W. (1938) Letter to M. Holmes, 28 February, *Board of Education papers*, National Archives, ED.136/2

Stradling, R. (1984) 'The teaching of controversial issues: an evaluation', *Educational Review*, Vol. 36, No. 2, pp. 121–9

Strand, T. (2009) 'The making of the new cosmopolitanism', *Studies in the Philosophy of Education* (online) Available from: uio.academia.edu/TorillStrand/Papers/163999/The_Making_of_a_New_Cosmopolitanism (accessed 16 July 2011)

Swann, M., Peacock, A., Hart, S. and Drummond, M. J. (2012 forthcoming) *Creating Learning without Limits*, Maidenhead: Open University Press

Swift, D. (2008) *Is Public Accountability Really the Global key to Quality Education?* (online). Available from: www.*home.hiroshima-u.ac.jp/cice/e-forum/101doc.pdf* (accessed 16 June 2011)

Tawney, R. H. (1938) *Equality*, London: Allen and Unwin

Tawney, R. H. (1943) Letter to Douglas Miller (Manchester Grammar School), 30 January, *Tawney papers*, Institute of Education: University of London

Taylor, C. and Robinson, C. (2009) 'Student voice: theorising power and participation', *Pedagogy, Culture and Society*, Vol. 17, No. 2, pp 161–75

Theoharis, G. (2007) *The School Leaders our Children Deserve: Seven Keys to Equity, Social Justice and School Reform*, New York: Teachers College Press

Thornberg, R. (2008) 'Values education as the daily fostering of school rules', *Research In Education*, Vol. 80, pp. 52–62

Torney-Purta, J., Barber, C. and Wilkenfeld, B. (2007) '"Latino adolescents" civic cevelopment in the United States: research results from the IEA Civic Education Study', *Journal of Youth and Adolescence*, Vol. 36, No. 2, pp. 111–25

Torney-Purta, J., Lehmann, R., Oswald, H. and Schulz, W. (2001) *Citizenship and Education in Twenty-Eight Countries*, Amsterdam: International Association for the Evaluation of Educational Achievement

Torney-Purta, J., Schwille, J. and Amadeo, J. (eds) (1999) *Civic Education Across Countries: Twenty-Four Case Studies*, Amsterdam: International Association for the Evaluation of Educational Achievement

Torres, C. A. (1998) 'Education, democracy and multiculturalism: dilemmas of citizenship in a global world'. Presidential address at annual meeting of the Comparative and International Education Society (CIES), March 17–21

Trafford, B. (2008) 'Democratic schools: towards a definition', in Arthur, J., Davies, I. and Hahn, C. (eds) (2008) *The Sage Handbook of Education for Citizenship and Democracy*, London: Sage, pp. 410–23

Tripp, D. (1998) 'Critical incidents in action enquiry', in Shacklock, G. and Smyth, J. (eds) (1998) *Being Reflexive in Critical Educational and Social Research*, London: Falmer Press, pp. 35–48

Tyack, D. and Cuban, L. (1995) *Tinkering Toward Utopia: A Century of Public School Reform*, Cambridge, MA: Harvard University Press

Verhellen, E. (2000) *Convention on the Rights of the Child*, Antwerp: Garant

Waghid, Y. (2009) 'Patriotism and democratic citizenship education in South Africa: on the (im) possibility of reconciliation and nation building', *Educational Philosophy & Theory*, Vol. 41, No. 4, pp. 399–409

Waks, L. J. (2008) 'Cosmopolitanism and citizenship education', in: Peters, M. A., Britton, A. and Blee, H. (eds) (2008) *Global Citizenship Education: Philosophy, Theory and Pedagogy*, Rotterdam: Sense, pp. 203–19

Walford, G. (ed.) (2003) *British Private Schools: Research on Policy and Practice*, London: Woburn

Watkins, C. (2006) 'Citizenship, leadership and the progressive public schools of interwar Britain', DPhil thesis, University of Oxford

Watts, J. (ed.) (1977) *The Countesthorpe Experience: The First Five Years*, London: Allen and Unwin

Whiteley, P. (2005) *Citizenship Education Longitudinal Study Second Literature Review: Citizenship Education: The Political Science Perspective*, DfES Research Report 631, Nottingham: DfES

Whitty, G. (2005) 'Education(al) research and education policy making: is conflict inevitable?', Inaugural Presidential Address British Education Research Association, University of Glamorgan, September 2005

Whitty, G. and Whisby, E. (2007) *Real Decision Making? School Councils in Action*, Annesley: DCSF

Williams, J. and Invernizzi, A. (eds) (2008) *Children and Citizenship*, London and Los Angeles: Sage

Williams, R. (1961) *The Long Revolution*, London: Chatto and Windus

Wolf, A. (2002) *Does Education Matter? Myths about Education and Economic Growth*, London: Penguin

Woodhead, C. (2002) *Class War: The State of Education*, London: Little, Brown

Young, I. M. (1989) 'Polity and group difference: a critique of the ideal of universal citizenship', *Ethics*, Vol. 99, No. 2, pp. 250–74

Zukin, C., Keeter, S., Andolina, M., Jenkins, K. and Delli Carpini, M. X. (2006) *A New Engagement? Political Participation, Civic Life, and the Changing American Citizen*, Oxford: Oxford University Press

Index

Index